The
Forensic
Historian

ALSO PUBLISHED BY M.E. SHARPE

The Historian's Toolbox:
A Student's Guide to the Theory and Craft of History
Third Edition

by Robert C. Williams

The Forensic Historian

Using Science to Reexamine the Past

Robert C. Williams

M.E.Sharpe
Armonk, New York
London, England

The EuroSlavic fonts used to create this work are © 1986–2013 Payne Loving Trust.
EuroSlavic is available from Linguist's Software, Inc.,
www.linguistsoftware.com, P.O. Box 580, Edmonds, WA 98020-0580 USA
tel (425) 775-1130.

Library of Congress Cataloging-in-Publication Data

Williams, Robert Chadwell, 1938–
  The forensic historian : using science to reexamine the past /
by Robert C. Williams.
    p. cm.
  Includes bibliographical references and index.
  ISBN 978-0-7656-3661-4 (hardcover : alk. paper)—ISBN 978-0-7656-3662-1
(pbk. : alk. paper) 1. Historiography—Methodology—Case studies.
2. Forensic science—Case studies. 3. World history. I. Title.
  D16.W619 2012
  907.2—dc23   2012033681

Printed in the United States of America

The paper used in this publication meets the minimum requirements of
American National Standard for Information Sciences
Permanence of Paper for Printed Library Materials,
ANSI Z 39.48-1984.

IBT (c) 10   9   8   7   6   5   4   3   2   1
SP (p) 10   9   8   7   6   5   4   3   2   1

I determine what happened, not whodunit.

—Michael Baden, medical examiner, City of New York

The evidence never lies.

—Herbert MacDonell, fingerprint expert

Bones make good witnesses. They may speak softly, but they don't lie and they never forget.

—Clyde Snow, forensic anthropologist

Contents

List of Illustrations and Table   ix
Preface: Mildred Trotter and the Boneyard of War   xi

1. Introduction: Scope of Evidence   **3**

1.1   Mikhail Gerasimov: Making Ivan the Terrible's Face   5

2. Faking It: Chemistry and Forgery   **10**

2.1   Paul Coremans: The Girl with the Bakelite Earring   10
2.2   Walter McCrone: Ink Testing the Vinland Map   16
2.3   Julius Grant: Ultraviolet Light on the Hitler Diaries   21
2.4   Walter McCrone Again: Carbon-14 Dating the Shroud
      of Turin   26
2.5   Philippe Charlier: The Bogus Remains of Joan of Arc   29
      References   31

3. Atomic Evidence   **33**

3.1   Sten Forshufvud: The Arsenic in Napoleon's Hair   34
3.2   Vincent Guinn: The "Magic Bullet" and the Kennedy
      Assassination   38
3.3   William Maples: The Death of Zachary Taylor   44
3.4   William Walsh: Testing Beethoven's Hair   48
      References   53

**4. A Question of Identity: From Bones to
DNA Fingerprinting**   **55**

4.1   Clyde Snow: Identifying the "Angel of Death"   57
4.2   Peter Gill: Romanov Bones and DNA Matches   62
4.3   Eugene Foster: Jefferson's Children   70
4.4   Jean-Jacques Cassiman: The Heart of the Last King
       of France   73
4.5   Linda Strausbaugh: Hitler's Skull   78
      References   83

5. Not-So-Cold Cases   **85**

5.1   Jeffrey Taubenberger: Tracking the Killer Virus of 1918   86
5.2   Tim Foecke and Jennifer McCarty: Testing the
       Titanic Rivets   92
5.3   Zahi Hawass: The CT Scans of King Tutankhamun   98
5.4   The U.S. Navy SEALs: Identifying Osama bin Laden   103
5.5   Tsutomu Shimomura: Catching Kevin Mitnick   108
      References   116

6. Conclusion: Modern Forensics and Historical Revision   **118**

Glossary   123
Bibliography   127
Index   131
About the Author   143

List of Illustrations and Table

Illustrations

P.1	Dr. Mildred Trotter, 1955	xii
1.1	Tsar Ivan the Terrible	8
2.1	Han van Meegeren	15
2.2	The Vinland Map	18
2.3	Konrad Kujau	24
2.4	The Shroud of Turin	28
2.5	Joan of Arc	31
3.1	Napoleon on St. Helena	35
3.2	The "Magic Bullet"	40
3.3	Zachary Taylor	45
3.4	Beethoven's Hair	50
4.1	Josef Mengele	60
4.2 a	The Romanov Family, 1913	64
4.2 b	Alec Jeffreys	67
4.3	Thomas Jefferson and Sally Hemings	71
4.4	Louis XVII's Heart	77
4.5	Hitler's Skull?	81
5.1	The Flu Virus of 1918–1919	88
5.2	The *Titanic* Rivets	94
5.3	Zahi Hawass	101
5.4	Osama bin Laden	106
5.5	Kevin Mitnick	110
6.1	Oetzi the Iceman	119

Table

3.1	The Bullet Fragments	41

Preface

Mildred Trotter and the Boneyard of War

Teaching at Washington University in St. Louis in the 1970s and 1980s, I came to know a remarkable woman and pioneer forensic historian and anthropologist. Dr. Mildred Trotter, or "Trott," as she was known, had struggled in the male-dominated world of modern medicine for decades before becoming a professor of anatomy at the Washington University Medical School. Like my wife, my mother, and my grandmother, Dr. Trotter was an "uncommon woman" graduate of Mount Holyoke College (Class of 1920) and a scientist of uncommon intelligence, dedication, perseverance, and humor. A woman scientist was a rare bird in those days, and Mildred was not only rare, but tough. She had to be.

Trott had arrived at the Washington University medical school in 1920 and never left. (She died in 1991 at the age of ninety-two.) In 1948 the university granted her a fourteen-month (unpaid) leave of absence to work as a medical anthropologist in the Central Identification Laboratory of the U.S. Army's Graves Registration Service at Schofield Barracks in Hawaii. Here she helped identify the remains of thousands of U.S. servicemen and servicewomen who had died in the Pacific war against Japan. She was always proud of the fact that her laboratory identified 94 percent of the remains it measured and analyzed. Authenticity was mandatory, and no remains were ever delivered to a family without positive identification and absolute certainty.

Much of Trott's work involved measuring bones, skulls, and teeth, matching them with dog tags or dog-tag imprints, dental records, and other information to identify the war dead. She worked in a massive building that was airy, light, and sanitary. Her colleagues formed a team of twenty-three people in 1949. Ninety-nine percent of the remains collected were skeletal. In time, Dr. Trotter discovered a quantitative

Illustration P.1   **Dr. Mildred Trotter, 1955**

Mildred Trotter was a pioneer in forensic anthropology who
identified servicemen from World War II by their long bones.
*(Becker Medical Library, Washington University School of
Medicine)*

relationship between the length of limbs and long bones—femurs, tibiae,
and fibulae—and the height of an individual. For example, for white
males, height was determined as the length of the femur x 2.38 + 61.4
centimeters; the length of the tibia x 2.52 + 78.62 centimeters; or the
length of the fibula x 2.68 + 71.78 centimeters. Other measurements
became standards in forensic pathology for determining race, height,
weight, age, and gender. They proved especially helpful in identifying
passengers from downed aircraft. If you knew how to listen, bones could
talk and even testify.

Mildred Trotter was my first contact with forensics and the way in
which modern science could reexamine the past in the context of history
and law under the glare of media attention. Her significant contributions to forensic pathology were recognized only after her retirement.
Her work in bringing closure to the grief of thousands of families who
had lost loved ones in war was barely remembered. She was a pioneer
woman in the male-dominated world of modern medical science. She
lived through a period when forensics became the essential toolbox of

criminal investigations, and techniques like neutron activation analysis and DNA fingerprinting supplemented the evidence of bones and teeth. Trott helped me understand the significance of forensics in studying the past long before CSI became a television staple.

This book is therefore dedicated to the memory of Dr. Mildred Trotter and her contributions to modern forensics, and thus to history. She was, in fact, a pioneer forensic historian.

Acknowledgments

I would like to acknowledge again the help and support of my M.E. Sharpe editor, Steve Drummond, who was as much of a moving force behind *The Forensic Historian* as he was for my previous book *The Historian's Toolbox*. Henrietta Toth, Kim Giambattisto, and Laurie Lieb were again superb copyeditors. Phil Cantelon provided the perspective and wisdom of another professional historian. Walter Grzyb of the Maine State Police offered necessary perspectives and information on forensics. Mandy Combest of the Chief Medical Examiner's Office in Louisville, Kentucky, provided me with materials on the 1991 exhumation of U.S. president Zachary Taylor. Amanda Walsh arranged for me to visit the new *Titanic* museum in Belfast that provided insights into the case of the *Titanic* rivets. My wife Ann, a gifted scientist, editor, and friend, inspired the title (again) and contributed some central ideas. None of them should be blamed for the shortcomings of a forensic history they helped craft.

Robert C. Williams
Center Lovell, Maine, 2012

References

A brief biography of Dr. Mildred Trotter and her 1949 report on "Operations at Central Identification Laboratory" may be found in the Bernard Becker Medical Library Digital Collection at Washington University in St. Louis, online at http://beckerexhibits.wustl.edu/mowihsp/words/TrotterReport.htm.

The
Forensic
Historian

Introduction

Scope of Evidence

History, as Edward Gibbon once pointed out, is in part the "register of the crimes, follies, and misfortunes of mankind." History is often a crime scene investigation in which the historian plays the role of a detective, perhaps even a medical examiner. Historians tell a story, and make an argument, that may be confirmed or altered by modern science and forensics, as well as by new evidence and interpretation. The forensic historian investigating past crimes engages in discovery and construction, science and art, the examination of evidence and the creation of narrative.

For historians, the scope of evidence has always been broad. Historians tend to utilize whatever evidence is at hand and whatever analytic approaches they believe could shed more light on that evidence.

Forensic historians examine cases that are relevant in a court of law or in public discussion and debate. (The word *forensic* derives from the Latin *forum*, the public square.) Forensics means the application of science to legal problems, in our case, problems from the past. Forensic historians apply science to questions of historical interest, debate, or argument that may also have legal implications. They may be trained historians utilizing forensic expertise and evidence, or trained forensic scientists examining cold cases from the past. There is as yet no real field of forensic history.

This book examines some famous historical criminal cases where modern forensic science investigators have tried to solve a mystery or revised accepted historical wisdom. It focuses on investigators who utilized analytic chemistry, neutron activation, carbon-14 dating, light and electron microscopy, ballistics, facial reconstruction, DNA fingerprinting, computer autopsies, and ultraviolet light fluorescence. Most cases examined by forensic historians involve:

- a *reasonable suspicion* that a crime or misdemeanor was committed
- a well-known *historical* figure or event that attracted media attention
- modern *forensic* techniques utilized to conduct historical research
- a *probable cause* to indict someone for committing a crime
- a historiographical *debate*—an argument without end—that has continued despite, or because of, new scientific results regarding the case.

Forensics, as we shall discover, does not necessarily close a case from the past, but may open new areas for debate and discussion. Forensic science provides new tools for the historian's toolbox, new ways of examining and investigating the grave evidence of the past. Documents and photographs, skulls and bones, hair and teeth, paint flakes and hard drives, ballistics and DNA analysis all may be brought to bear on a case. Since World War II, forensic pathology and anthropology have slowly given way to genetics and DNA "fingerprinting," along with computer hardware and software, as scientific evidence that can stand up in court. This book highlights that transition through specific case studies showing how modern forensic historians and scientists do their work and what kinds of evidence they must obtain.

These historical cases are organized around the forensic work of the scientists who investigated them, often long after the fact. The book begins with the man who reconstructed the face of Ivan the Terrible in 1953 and ends with the team that confirmed the death of Osama bin Laden by DNA analysis in 2011. During that period—and especially after the invention of DNA fingerprinting in 1985—a small group of men and women traveled the globe seeking to apply forensics to history. Initially forensic pathologists and anthropologists working on bones, they became specialists in extracting DNA from old, even ancient, bodies in order to answer questions of paternity, identity, and genealogy.

Case open or case closed, modern forensics provides crucial tools, evidence, and perspectives on the past. Forensics broadens the scope of evidence for the historian. As forensic pathologist William Maples pointed out, dead men do tell tales. History reaches us not simply through the dead hand of the past, but through the living hands and eyes of modern scientists. And science less often closes cases than it adds a valuable and exciting new dimension to historical debate. Although the media tend to exaggerate the novelty in these cases and to oversimplify scientific research, they indicate just how fascinated the public is with forensic approaches to history.

Or as forensic anthropologist Clyde Snow put it, "Bones make good witnesses. They may speak softly, but they don't lie and they never forget." So it is with DNA fingerprints.

1.1 Mikhail Gerasimov: Making Ivan the Terrible's Face

Forensic historians are both artists and scientists. We begin with the work of Soviet forensic anthropologist Mikhail Gerasimov (1907–1970) because his forensic history involved both art and science, the reconstruction of faces from skulls and the measurement of skulls and bones necessary to the task. He used science to investigate the past and art to re-create it.

In 1953 the Soviets buried one criminal and exhumed another. Joseph Stalin, a native of Georgia and the totalitarian dictator of the Soviet Union, died in March, having been responsible for the imprisonment, torture, and murder of millions of people over several decades through his policies of collectivization of the peasantry, purges of the Communist Party and the army, slave labor camps, and forced industrialization of the USSR. World War II slaughtered millions more Soviet citizens. How many people did Stalin murder? No one really knows the exact number, but 30 million people is not a bad guess.

A few weeks after Stalin's death, on April 23, 1953, a special commission of the Ministry of Culture opened the sarcophagus of Ivan the Terrible—Tsar Ivan IV (1530–1584), or John the Dread, as British historians dubbed him—to conduct a scientific, historical, and forensic analysis of his remains in the Archangel Cathedral of the Kremlin in Moscow. Like the nearby tombs of his two sons, Fedor and Ivan, Ivan the Terrible's tomb was constructed of brick, covered with plaster, and then overlaid with bronze. The three graves had never previously been disturbed. Ivan's victims numbered in the thousands, not millions, but everyone knew him as a ruler who enjoyed torturing and murdering his recalcitrant subjects, especially the landed nobility, known as boyars.

Why open the tomb of Ivan the Terrible, Stalin's hero among Russian rulers? Ivan had been a cult figure under Stalin, who considered Ivan his teacher, a "great and wise ruler" surrounded by hostile foreigners and wealthy boyars. Ivan was the subject of one of movie director Sergei Eisenstein's greatest films. In 1947 Stalin told Eisenstein that Ivan's only mistake was not to liquidate everyone who opposed him. Stalin had come close to doing just that. Now Stalin was dead, and curiosity could at last be satisfied by forensics. Perhaps the scientists opened Ivan's tomb simply because they finally could do so without fear for their careers—and their lives. Or perhaps they were carrying out Stalin's own orders—posthumously.

A key member of the team exhuming the body of Ivan was Mikhail Gerasimov, a well-known forensic anthropologist, archaeologist, and pioneer of facial reconstruction based on skulls and skeletons. Born in St. Petersburg in 1907, Gerasimov had studied forensic medicine and anthropology at Irkutsk and Moscow in the 1920s. He measured skulls, bones, and the soft tissue in corpses to attempt to reconstruct the faces of individuals. Since the average thickness of soft tissue and muscle was known for types of individuals, pegs of varying lengths (now called tissue-thickness markers) were placed around the skull at various points and covered with rubber sheeting to begin facial reconstruction.

Gerasimov had worked as a scientific technical assistant at the Irkutsk Museum in the 1920s, reconstructing faces from Neanderthal and Pithecanthropus fossils, and became a "doctor of facial science." He took on a number of criminal cases for Stalin's police, the dreaded NKVD, and began reconstructing the faces of famous historical figures, including Dostoevsky's mother, Alexander the Great, and early Kievan ruler Andrei Bogoliubsky. In the 1890s, Swiss-born anatomist Wilhelm His had created models of faces from skulls (notably composer Johann Sebastian Bach), and in the 1930s the FBI tried some facial reconstruction in the United States. But Gerasimov took this early work to another level.

In June 1941, Gerasimov helped excavate the Mongol emperor Tamerlane's tomb and began to reconstruct Tamerlane's face from skull fragments found. Tamerlane's name meant "Timur the Lame," and his bones confirmed his disability. Opening Tamerlane's tomb, the local residents believed, would bring down a curse upon those responsible. Indeed, on June 22—the day Gerasimov opened the tomb—Hitler's armies invaded the Soviet Union. Many local residents believe to this day that World War II was in part the consequence of Tamerlane's curse.

During the rest of the war, Gerasimov worked at the medical hospital in Tashkent on war victims. Like Mildred Trotter, he had ample opportunity to measure precisely the costs of combat on the human body.

In 1953 the bones of Ivan the Terrible showed a man wracked by pain who relieved his own torment by tormenting others. What did the Soviet Union's Research Institute of Forensic Medicine add to what historians already knew about Ivan?

Ivan's skeleton was covered with the torn pieces of a monk's robe, confirming that immediately after his death Ivan was tonsured as the monk Jonah. His bones were well preserved but brittle, showing traces of quicksilver and arsenic. The arsenic was within the normal range, but the mercury content was unusually high. Ivan was taller than believed at six feet. He was also heavier than believed, weighing 210 pounds when he died. Ivan's bones showed osteophytes, indicating that he had polyarthritis and was in constant and severe pain. His cartilages and ligaments had ossified, indicating that he had used mercury ointment to alleviate his pain.

Ivan's bones showed what contemporary records did not: that he was indeed terrible (or awful, or dreaded, as implied by the Russian word *groznyi*) not only because of his acts of terror, sadism, and cruelty, but because of his unusual height. They also indicated a man wracked by physical pain and subject to the ministrations of doctors. They did not suggest that Ivan was poisoned or otherwise murdered.

In his 1572 last will and testament, Ivan confessed to a corrupt spirit and a "liking for unworthy things." He had indulged in "murder, lewdness and other bad acts," along with self-praise, pride, and arrogance. He also admitted to "theft and assassination," not to mention "shamelessness, debauchery and drinking." And he had a "readiness to commit all sorts of evil." Ivan's own last will and testament painted quite a self-portrait of a man terrible indeed. Gerasimov's facial reconstruction from the skull matched contemporary descriptions of Ivan. But until Gerasimov's reconstruction, historians had no idea what Ivan actually looked like except from the marvelous but speculative portraits by later Russian painters. (Gerasimov deserved the extra month's salary he received for his work.)

Gerasimov's techniques became high tech. A skull was set on a turntable, exposed to a low-power laser beam, the contours recorded by a video camera and the results fed into a computer for manipulation. Computer information was then fed into a milling machine that produced a three-dimensional portrait of the individual in hard foam. Today facial reconstruction amounts to three-dimensional modeling by computer, using CT scanners to reconstruct the axial sections of a

Illustration 1.1   **Tsar Ivan the Terrible**

Ivan the Terrible was Gerasimov's most famous facial reconstruction, based on his exhumed body.

skull target on film. The results are fed into a computer and sometimes compared with another photograph. The resultant pictures amount to a virtual autopsy.

The art of facial reconstruction is now standard procedure, used by film makeup artists and forensic investigators alike. Facial reconstruction—like history—combines both art and science. To re-create the past with accuracy and imagination requires us to utilize the discoveries and techniques of science, while recognizing that we ultimately construct, as well as discover, the events and personalities of the past. Facial reconstruction, like history, can at best approximate the vanished past.

Ivan the Terrible was a major criminal of the sixteenth century. Now, because of Gerasimov's facial reconstruction, we have a good idea what he looked like. But Gerasimov and his team had been limited by the traditional tools of forensic pathology in their examination of the bones of Ivan the Terrible. On April 25, 1953, the journal *Nature* published three papers explaining for the first time the double-helical structure of DNA, the building blocks of life. Only the revolution in molecular biology engendered by the discovery of the structure of DNA would provide in the 1980s an entirely novel toolbox allowing forensic historians to investigate the crimes of the past.

If he were alive today, Mikhail Gerasimov would know that Ivan the Terrible, a descendant of the Viking conqueror of Kiev, Riurik, belonged to the Y-DNA haplogroup N (N1c1) and was descended from Swedes. Joseph Stalin, by genetic testing of his grandson and grandnephew, was Y-DNA-wise a G2a1. Modern forensics has moved from chemistry, anthropology, and pathology of bones to the genetic study of DNA "fingerprints" and the analysis of computer hardware and software. How did this transformation come about?

References

On Gerasimov, see M.M. Gerasimov, *The Face Finder*, trans. A.H. Brodrick (Philadelphia: J.B. Lippincott, 1971); and John Prag and Richard Neave, *Making Faces: Using Forensic and Archaeological Evidence* (London: British Museum Press, 1997).

Faking It

Chemistry and Forgery

1945: Europe lay in ruins after World War II. Forgery and other wartime deceptions flourished on both sides of the conflict. In Amsterdam, chemist Paul Coremans listened incredulously as Dutch painter Han van Meegeren explained how he had swindled Hermann Göring and other top Nazis with bogus artworks by "Old Masters." In the devastated Munich suburb of Pullach rested the papers of Father Josef Fischer, an anti-Nazi Jesuit cartographer who left behind a fake "Vinland Map" of the North Atlantic satirizing Nazi dreams of Aryan domination. A young British intelligence officer, Hugh Trevor-Roper, interviewed the Nazi survivors of Hitler's underground bunker in Berlin for stories of his last days and suicide, an attempt by MI6 to show that Hitler was really dead. In northern Italy, King Umberto II of the House of Savoy returned the venerated Catholic relic, the Shroud of Turin, to that city after hiding it from the Nazi occupiers in the Benedictine monastery of Monte Vergine, south of Rome. And in Paris, resistance leader Charles de Gaulle proclaimed himself the successor to Saint Joan of Arc and her Cross of Lorraine his national symbol of France. All across Europe, black markets flourished in a devastated economy, and one of their most valuable commodities was forgery.

For forensic historians, the crime of forgery raises questions of authenticity that can only be answered by science: How old is the object in question? What materials were used in its construction? Was one painting done on top of another? If it is a forgery, has the forger confessed?

2.1 Paul Coremans: The Girl with the Bakelite Earring

By 1947 Paul Coremans knew for certain that the paintings were forged. The Belgian chemist had learned in his laboratory that the Dutch forger and painter Han van Meegeren had used twentieth-century Bakelite to harden paint on his supposedly seventeenth-century Vermeers. In addition, by the time Coremans got to testify in court, Meegeren readily admitted to the crime of forgery in order to escape trial for the much more serious crime of collaboration with the Nazis. Science confirmed what the criminal—a chronic liar—had already told the scientists, showing that a liar can sometimes tell the truth, for his own good.

Analyzing and proving the authenticity (or not) of a painting was already a highly technical matter of paint, paint chips, canvas, and wormholes. The chemistry of paint, in particular, could show whether or not a particular painting was of the time and place claimed. Coremans knew he was dealing with a twentieth-century forger even before van Meegeren confessed to the crime—and showed the jury how he did it.

Paul B. Coremans (1908–1965) had a distinguished career at the intersection of art and chemistry. Born in Borgerhout, Belgium, Coremans was too young to serve in World War I. He received his PhD in analytical chemistry from the University of Brussels in 1932 and two years later set up his own laboratory at the Royal Museum of Art and History. In 1937, on his first trip to the United States, he visited the art conservation laboratory at the Fogg Art Museum at Harvard University. By the time World War II broke out, Coremans was director of the Royal Institute for the Study and Conservation of Belgium's Artistic Heritage and one of the leading art conservators in the world.

During World War II, Coremans led a team that photographed monuments and art throughout Belgium, documenting the ravages of war and the claims of owners whose art was looted by the Nazis. In 1945 he joined the U.S. "Monuments Men" engaged in identifying, rescuing, and repatriating thousands of artworks stolen by the Nazis. Coremans was particularly interested in the case of Han van Meegeren, a notorious forger of art arrested by the Americans in Amsterdam in May 1945 after one of his fake Vermeers was discovered in Nazi leader Hermann Göring's house. Charged with selling Dutch cultural property and therefore collaboration with the enemy, van Meegeren faced the death penalty for treason. So he promptly changed his plea to forgery, which he readily admitted.

Han van Meegeren was born in 1889 in Deventer, the Netherlands, and given the forbidding name Henricus Antonius van Meegeren. His father, a schoolteacher and disciplinarian, once compelled his son to write 100 times on a sheet of paper, "I know nothing, I am nothing, I am capable of nothing." Later the unsupportive father wrote his son lovingly, "You are a cheat and always will be."

Fascinated by art at an early age, van Meegeren learned from his mentor, Bartus Korteling, how the great artist Johannes Vermeer (1632–1675) mixed and made his own colors of paint for his palette. From 1907 to 1913, van Meegeren studied architecture in Delft, Vermeer's hometown. He even designed a boathouse for his rowing club. But in 1913 van Meegeren abandoned architecture for painting and drawing. A year later he moved to Schevingen with his young wife, Anna de Voogt. In the spring of 1917, he had his first painting exhibition in The Hague and by 1919 was a well-established portrait painter. After travels to England, France, Belgium, and Italy, he divorced Anna in 1923 and turned to a much more lucrative career that would make him famous—forgery.

At first van Meegeren began painting in the style of Franz Hals, another well-known seventeenth-century Dutch artist. The fact that he was basically copying Hals paintings, as many art students were encouraged to do, was not lost on the critics. As one said of van Meegeren, "he has every virtue except originality."

In 1930, impoverished by the Great Depression and alienated from the art world and its critics, van Meegeren moved to the south of France and began forging works by Hals, Vermeer, Pieter de Hooch, and Gerhard ter Borch, all well-known Dutch painters. Slowly he began to sell his forgeries through a series of agents. In 1936 he triumphed when the famous art expert Abraham Bredius accepted his fake Vermeer, *The Supper at Emmaus*, as a real Vermeer. (There are only about thirty-five Vermeer paintings in the world that are known to be genuine.) Van Meegeren sold the painting to the Rembrandt Society for 520,000 guilders, over $4 million today. And he went off to see his hero, Adolf Hitler, preside over the Berlin Olympic Games.

Van Meegeren's techniques were impressive. He purchased seventeenth-century canvas from antique dealers; mixed his own paints from lapis lazuli, white lead, indigo, and cinnabar as Vermeer had; made badger-hair paintbrushes like Vermeer's; and used a mixture of phenol and formaldehyde, with some wood filler, baked slowly in an oven, to harden the paint. He also added some turpentine and linseed oil, later lavender or lilac oil. The mixture was in fact an early plastic known as Bakelite, and it would ultimately provide his undoing.

Van Meegeren first used Bakelite in his 1932 painting *The Gentleman and Lady at the Spinet*. Bakelite at the time was a plastic used for telephones, costume jewelry, radios, toys, and kitchenware. It had a hard, tough finish, did not conduct electricity, and did not soften in water. It was basically carbolic acid and liquid formaldehyde hardened by baking. Van Meegeren simply ground his replicated pigments into liquid Bakelite and then applied them to seventeenth-century canvas. He then rolled the result over his knees to produce simulated cracking.

Leo Baekeland, a Belgian chemist, had developed this early plastic sometime around 1907. In 1899 he made his first million dollars by inventing a new photographic paper for the Kodak Company. He soon moved to New York, where he established his own laboratory and formed the Bakelite Corporation in 1922. Bakelite was in use in many products throughout the 1920s and 1930s. (Today there are even Bakelite museums in Ghent and Amsterdam that trace the history of the first plastic.) Baekeland himself appeared on the cover of *Time* magazine in September 1924 with the cryptic caption, "It will not burn, it will not melt."

By 1938 Van Meegeren's forgeries were sufficiently marketable that he could afford to move to Nice on the French Riviera and acquire a twelve-room mansion. On the eve of the war, he moved back to Amsterdam, continued his forgery career, and became addicted to morphine. In 1942 one of his agents sold a "Vermeer" titled *Christ with the Adultress* to the art dealer Alois Miedl, who in turn sold it to Nazi leader Hermann Göring for 1.65 million guilders, equivalent to some $7 million today. The painting soon joined Göring's other artworks at his estate named Carinhall, and then was shipped off to Austrian salt mines with looted Nazi art to be protected from Allied bombing raids.

In May 1945, the Allies questioned Miedl as a collaborator and imprisoned him. They also arrested van Meegeren and questioned him. After three days in jail for collaboration, he soon confessed to forgery. "Idiots!" he cried at one point; "You think I sold a Vermeer to that fat Göring. But it's not a Vermeer. I painted it myself." Kept under arrest until February 1946, van Meegeren talked at length about his forgery techniques and career. He even painted a "Vermeer" in front of court-appointed witnesses to show how he had done it.

One of these witnesses was Paul Coremans, who interviewed van Meegeren at length and took x-rays of several of his claimed forgeries. Van Meegeren showed Coremans his paint and brushes and explained how he used Bakelite as a paint hardener. In July 1946, the court swore in Coremans and six other experts (four other scientists and two art historians) as a commission to conduct an official inquest into van

Meegeren's forgeries—specifically, eight "Vermeers" and "Hals" paintings. Coremans served as the chair. The scientists soon found traces of Bakelite in the paint, along with another plastic bonding agent known as Albertol, a phenolformaldehyde resin. A bottle of this twentieth-century chemical was located in van Meegeren's studio. The experts also confirmed that India ink had been used to simulate grime in the cracks, and they identified cobalt blue paint, first used in the nineteenth century and unavailable to Vermeer in his day.

Van Meegeren's forgery trial began on October 29, 1947, in Amsterdam in Room 4 of the Regional Court. Some 200 spectators and journalists jammed the courtroom. The court had dropped collaboration charges on the grounds that Göring's "Vermeer" was not Dutch cultural property, but van Meegeren's own creation. Prosecutor H.A. Wassenbergh read off the forgery and fraud charges, asking that the defendant receive a sentence of two years in prison. Paul Coremans began the trial with a scientific lecture and slide show on craquelure (paint cracking), Bakelite, x-rays, and other technical issues. The courtroom audience was mesmerized. Van Meegeren himself was duly impressed. "Outstanding work, your honor," he told the judge regarding Coremans's testimony; "very well done." The admiration was mutual—Coremans later admitted that van Meegeren was "indisputably the greatest forger of all time."

On November 12, the court found van Meegeren guilty of forgery and fraud, sentencing him to a year in prison. The forger suffered one heart attack, on November 26, then another on December 29. He died in prison on December 30, a bankrupt man and perhaps the greatest forger of the modern era. He had told Coremans that September that his main purpose was vengeance on the art world that had originally rejected his work.

But Coremans was not finished. In 1949 he published a book on the science confirming van Meegeren's forgeries titled *Van Meegeren's Faked Vermeers and de Hooghs: A Scientific Examination*. In it he showed how microscopes and spectroscopes revealed the layers of paint over an old canvas, the visible "age crackle" of a forgery, and the presence of pigment chemicals unknown in the seventeenth century—cobalt blue, ultramarine, and modern white lead. He realized that, despite the technicalities, "the detection of the synthetic resin medium found in all the fakes will be appreciated by all." Van Meegeren painted with Bakelite.

Two years later another Brussels art expert wrote in a book that Coremans was wrong and that at least two of the "Vermeers" were authentic.

Illustration 2.1 **Han van Meegeren**

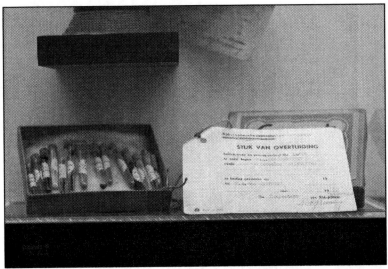

Modern paint pigments helped convict the forger Han van Meegeren, but only after he confessed to forgery and showed a jury how he had done it.

The buyer of the two paintings in question promptly sued Coremans. A trial was scheduled for June 2, 1955, but the plaintiff died. When his heirs brought suit, the case went to court and Coremans won.

In 1967 two scientists at the Artists Materials Center at Carnegie-Mellon University in Pittsburgh, Robert Feller and Bernard Keisch, confirmed that Coremans had been correct in ascribing the "Vermeers" to van Meegeren. Seventeenth-century Dutch white lead turned out to have a much higher content of silver and antinomy than modern white lead. Pb 210 lead decayed radioactively from U-238 with a half-life of 22.3 years. The trace elements of polonium and radium in the white lead could be measured by their decay rate, again providing the modern dating of van Meegeren's work.

Likewise, in 1977, the state forensic laboratory in the Netherlands utilized gas chromatography to confirm six "Vermeer" forgeries and thus to reaffirm the chemical results of Coremans. Finally, in 2010, Scotland Yard released a file on van Meegeren showing that in 1931 he bought a large supply of ultramarine and lapis lazuli pigment from the British art firm Winsor and Newton, enough to keep him in the forgery business for a number of years. The British investigated him not because he was a forger, but because he appeared to be a Nazi collaborator.

Han van Meegeren died a hero in Holland, a cunning trickster who had fooled the Nazis into thinking they were looting authentic master-pieces. Even the paintings by the known master forger himself found success in the art market, exhibited in famous museums and sold as van Meegerens to eager buyers. If they could not buy a Vermeer, at least they could afford a van Meegeren. In this case, the forensics tests of Paul Coremans and others simply corroborated what the forger himself admitted. Forensics did not revise history, but confirmed it. The dead witness had for once in his life told the truth—fortunately to the Dutch police and not the Nazi Gestapo. And the inert painting testified to the miracle of Bakelite and the skill of the forger.

2.2 Walter McCrone: Ink Testing the Vinland Map

Not accidentally, Yale University Press announced on Columbus Day—October 11, 1965—that it had acquired and would publish a previously unknown map of the world from the fifteenth century. The so-called Vinland Map was bound together with a text known as *The Tatar Relation*, or *Hystoria Tartarum*. Vinland, or Wineland, was apparently a medieval name given to present-day Greenland or Cape Breton on Nova Scotia.

Perhaps Yale was rushed into this announcement by the discovery in November 1964 of L'Anse aux Meadow in Newfoundland, where the Vikings or Norsemen were discovered to have landed in America centuries before Columbus. President Lyndon Johnson promptly declared October 9 to be Leif Eriksson Day, after the famous Norse explorer, three days ahead of Columbus Day, October 12 that year. Italian-Americans were understandably upset at the Yale announcement a year later of a map suggesting that the Vikings, not an Italian, had discovered America.

Everything about the provenance of the map seemed secret or questionable. Yale would admit only that the map had been "acquired from a private collection in Europe" by Laurence C. Witten (1926–1995), a book dealer from Southport, Connecticut, who had donated numerous old and rare books to Yale in the past. Witten had no particular expertise regarding maps and said only that he had purchased the Vinland Map in 1957 from Enzo Ferrajoli de Ry, a retired Italian army officer and book dealer who had the reputation of a con man. Witten had met him two years earlier. Personally eccentric, Ferrajoli "ran" rare books and manuscripts around Europe in the trunk of his Fiat Topolino in the 1950s. The items rarely arrived with any evidence of provenance, or history of ownership, and Ferrajoli would say only that they came "from various libraries and collections."

Ferrajoli was indeed a charming con man. Among his many customers after the war was Maria Jose of Belgium, the last queen of Italy, now living in Swiss exile. She was the first member of the Italian royal family to contact the Allies about surrender terms in 1944. In 1957 Ferrajoli was convicted of stealing hundreds of rare books and manuscripts from the Cathedral of La See in Saragossa and sentenced to eight years in prison.

The media smelled a rat. On March 6, 1966, the London *Times* asked, "Is the *Vinland Map* a forgery?" Two British experts on old maps, Eva Taylor and Helen Wallis, came to doubt its authenticity after they saw the map. Nobody consulted them, while the Yale experts proclaimed that the map was authentic. Bertram Schofield, keeper of manuscripts at the British Museum, had first seen the Vinland Map in 1957 and refused to recommend its purchase.

The map itself was curious. The design was asymmetrical, a double-paged parchment some eleven by sixteen inches with a crude center strip holding the pages together. The pages had two different styles of handwriting on the map. The usual notation "earthly paradise" was missing. The details suggested the influence of medieval Christianity and the dream of Catholic global hegemony. There were wormholes and the ink was unevenly faded.

The *Tatar Relation* was a Franciscan friar's intelligence report on the Mongol empire dated July 30, 1247, and signed "C. de Bridia," a name unknown to experts and appearing nowhere else on the map, nor in any other map. Sensibly, Yale alumnus Paul Mellon (1907–1999) agreed to purchase the map in 1959 but would not donate it to the Beinecke Rare Book Library at Yale until it was authenticated. He also kept his purchase of the map a secret. Only in 1964, after much mystery and secrecy, did the three experts selected by Yale concur that the map was indeed authentic. Skepticism persisted, however, fueled by the knowledge that Mellon and many of the others involved had served with the U.S. Office of Strategic Services (OSS) in London during the war. Some thought Mellon still worked for the CIA as late as 1968. Was the map a product of Yale World War II spooks having some fun?

Illustration 2.2   **The Vinland Map**

A section of the Vinland Map showing parts of Europe and North America.

Amid the furor, a Vinland Map conference held at Yale in November 1966 recommended that the map be studied "scientifically" to determine its age, authorship, and authenticity. To do so, Yale agreed to ask the well-known Chicago specialist in forensics, analytical chemistry, and crystallography, Walter McCrone (1916–2002), to examine the map. The Vinland Map thus became an object of study by scientists and forensic historians.

McCrone was well qualified. He had received both his BA and PhD degrees from Cornell University in chemistry. In 1956 he had founded McCrone Associates with his wife Lucy to provide especially polarized light microscopy services to clients seeking to determine the chemical composition of unknowns. In the case of the Vinland Map, Yale in 1972 asked McCrone to examine the black and yellow ink on the parchment, using tiny samples lifted from the map. A Yale librarian brought the map to McCrone's laboratory in Chicago for examination and sampling. A microscopist, Anna Teestov, took twenty-nine ink and parchment samples.

A quick glance at the map produced doubts in McCrone's mind. The ink lines on the map were double: a broad yellow line and a narrow black line within it. The yellow pigment would be the key to the question of a forgery.

After a year or two of painstaking analysis with a light microscope, McCrone found some problematic results. In the 1400s, the supposed date of the map, mapmakers used India ink made from soot and iron-gall ink made from oak burls. The India ink was stable, but the iron-gall ink rusted over time to become a yellow-fringed ferrous oxide (Fe_2O_3). McCrone concluded that a forger living in the twentieth century had used India ink and added yellow pigments to simulate age. Chemical analysis showed that the yellow was not rust, but synthetic anatase or titanium dioxide (TiO_2), patented in 1916 and first made available in 1920. (Anatase was available as a mineral in 1440, but not in its finely ground commercial form until 1920.) Years later, in 2001, McCrone again tested the ink and found the Raman spectrum of India ink and yellow anatase on the parchment, showing none of the embrittlement or discoloration produced by iron-gall ink. Yale was amazed and disbelieving.

In 1974 British cartographer Helen Wallis chaired a Royal Geographic Society symposium on the Vinland Map and again questioned the map's authenticity. She suggested that it might well be a joke or a tease, a playful construction by a skilled cartographer and historian who knew a lot about old maps and their inks, wormholes, and parchments. McCrone reiterated his conviction that the map was a twentieth-century forgery in an article in *Analytic Chemistry* in 1976.

In 1985 scientist Thomas Cahill of the Crocker Nuclear Laboratory at the University of California, Davis, used PIXE (Particle-Induced X-Ray Emission) to examine the Vinland Map. He found that titanium oxide was not a major part of the ink, but only trace amounts. (Cahill's samples were much larger than McCrone's.) Since Cahill's results appeared to contradict McCrone, Yale promptly sought Cahill's second opinion. McCrone responded in 1988 with a complete, published account of his 1974 results, arguing that the Cahill tests did not invalidate them. In fact, PIXE could identify titanium but not titanium dioxide.

In 1995 Kirsten Seaver—a historian of medieval Norse culture and fellow of the Royal Geographical Society—argued that the Vinland Map was indeed a modern forgery and that she had identified the probable forger, an Austrian Jesuit priest named Father Josef Fischer, who had died in 1944. Neither Seaver nor McCrone were invited to contribute to a lavish second edition of *The Vinland Map and the Tatar Relation* published that year by Yale University Press. (The more favorably inclined Thomas Cahill was invited instead.) Nor were McCrone and Seaver invited to attend the February 10, 1996, conference in New Haven where the map was displayed under armed guard and insured for an inflated value of $25 million. McCrone showed up uninvited anyway and handed out to participants his own unpublished paper titled "The Vinland Map: Still a Twentieth-Century Fake." The Yale contingent was not amused to have a skunk at its garden party.

After three decades of secrecy, Yale finally admitted that the anonymous donor of the Vinland Map was indeed Paul Mellon.

In 1999 McCrone returned to the fray by publishing in his own journal *Microscope* the results of his more recent study of the map. He had examined samples of the yellow ink liner from the map using a polarized light microscope to confirm the presence of synthetic anatase. He also found that the reddish fringe was not rust but a collagen tempera. Three years later, another scientist complicated the situation with radiocarbon dating: D.J. Donahue found that the parchment of the Vinland Map indeed could be dated from the years 1423–1445, but that it had been coated with some substance in the 1950s. In 2004 the analytic chemist Robin Clark supported McCrone's 1974 results using Raman microscopy: the particle size and distribution of the ink was characteristic of synthetic anatase, not iron-gall ink.

Kirsten Seaver finally published the results of her historical and cartographic research in a book in 2007, summing up the long-standing debate over the Vinland Map and concluding that the forger was in all probability Josef Fischer, S.J. (1858–1944), a famous Austrian cartographer. Ordained to the priesthood in 1890, Father Fischer taught at the Stella Matutina, a Jesuit boarding school in Austria. He published a well-known book called *The Discoveries of the Norsemen in America* in 1902. President Theodore Roosevelt wrote Fischer a letter of congratulations after receiving a copy of the book.

Stella Matutina suffered predictably under the Nazi occupation in the 1930s. In 1934 the Nazis closed the school, sent the students off to Switzerland, and kept the faculty from granting degrees, meeting in public, or publishing articles. Fischer himself, now in his eighties, finally took refuge in a castle during the war, then at a Jesuit foundation in Pullach near Munich, with all of his papers. Fischer died in October 1944, and after the war Pullach became the headquarters of a CIA-sponsored German spy organization that later formed the basis of the West German intelligence services. How the Vinland Map might have made its way from Pullach to Ferrajoli remains a mystery.

Josef Fischer had the means to forge the map. He was a world-class expert on old Norse maps and exploration, understood the relevant cartography and history, and had access to fifteenth-century parchment at Stella Matutina. His handwriting was consistent with that on the map. He had time on his hands and little teaching to do under the Nazi occupation, so he had opportunity. Finally, he had motive to create a map that would satirize and undermine Nazi ideology and its theory of the arctic origins of the Aryan race by showing the extent of Catholic influence in the North Atlantic. Forgery was Fischer's arcane way of resisting and sabotaging the Nazi assault on civilization and the Catholic Church. Although Fischer was not alive to confess his forgery, modern scholarship and forensic history strongly suggest that he indeed created the Vinland Map.

Forensics thus played a crucial role in demolishing historical and cartographic claims that the Vinland map was authentic. In particular, analytic chemistry showed that the ink used on the map was a twentieth-century product, even if the parchment and wormholes might have dated from the fifteenth century. Just as the discovery of Bakelite in van Meegeren forgeries confirmed his own story of faking Vermeers, so the discovery of anatase in the Vinland Map ink confirmed a twentieth-century origin of a supposedly late medieval document. But it took a historian to find the forger who made the map.

World War II created an entire universe of deceptions intended to win the war and fool the enemy. Van Meegeren wished to avoid execution for treason by showing how he had fooled the Nazis with fake paintings. Josef Fischer showed a similar desire to fool them with a fake map showing medieval Catholic expansion in the very area treasured by Nazi "Aryan" ideologies. Both forgers probably utilized similar inks and paints from Winsor and Newton in London. In so doing, they unwittingly displayed to modern forensic historians the contemporary materials used to create ostensibly old artifacts. Van Meegeren's forgeries and the Vinland Map should be viewed in the context of the Nazi occupation of Europe. So should another great postwar forgery, the "Hitler Diaries."

2.3 Julius Grant: Ultraviolet Light on the Hitler Diaries

Sometimes even eminent historians can be wrong, really wrong. In 1983 Sir Hugh Trevor-Roper, Lord Dacre, the preeminent historian of modern Britain, authenticated the sensational "Hitler Diaries" launched by a West German publisher, *Stern* magazine. Having duly examined the handwritten notebooks bound in leather for a few hours in a Zurich bank, Trevor-Roper returned to England with breathless news that the diaries appeared authentic. Only later did the historian discover that his MI6 coworker, Julius Grant, had utilized fluorescent light to figure out in a few hours that the diaries were yet another modern forgery that could not have been produced in Hitler's lifetime. In this case forensics quickly corrected a historian's embarrassing mistake caused by the lure of money and the feeding frenzy of journalists. A forensic historian would have known better.

On April 1, 1983, Trevor-Roper received a telephone call at his country home in Scotland from an editor at the *Sunday Times* informing him that the West German magazine *Stern* had obtained previously unknown diaries allegedly written by Adolf Hitler. Trevor-Roper was immediately skeptical, knowing that Germany was awash with fake Nazi memorabilia and forgeries. But *Stern* wanted to sell foreign serial rights to publish its sensational discovery and Rupert Murdoch, owner of the *Sunday Times*, was contemplating bidding on these rights. Trevor-Roper was a director of Murdoch's publishing operation. Would Lord Dacre be willing to fly to Zurich and examine some of the diaries? He would, in exchange for a five-figure fee (which he later apologetically refused to accept).

A week later, on April 8, Trevor-Roper saw about twenty pages of copies of the diaries at a Heathrow airport, but no originals. After taking some notes on the plane and arriving at the Handelsbank in Zurich, he saw fifty-eight leather-bound notebooks stacked up on a table in a back room at the bank. Each notebook had a red wax seal with the German eagle and the Gothic initials "A.H." in Old German script. The lined pages were filled with Germanic handwriting in black ink. "My doubts gradually dissolved," attested the historian; "I am now satisfied that the documents are authentic." Standard accounts of Hitler might well have to be revised. Among the many problems was the embarrassing fact that Trevor-Roper—like most Germans—could not even read the Old High German script, even if he had time to do so. His German was largely self-taught. And never mind that the director of the German Bundesarchiv in Koblenz had announced that the diaries were simply "eine plumpe Falschung," a crude forgery.

The next day, Murdoch arrived, leafed through the notebooks and promptly offered £3 million for world rights to their publication. The eminent historian's quick judgment was good enough to allow the publisher to bid.

On April 17, Trevor-Roper was surprised to learn that negotiations between *Stern* and the *Sunday Times* had collapsed. He promptly flew to Hamburg to meet the *Stern* reporter Gerd Heidemann, who showed him hundreds more Hitler photographs and documents. On April 21, Trevor-Roper published an article in the *Times* proclaiming the Hitler Diaries "an archive of great historical significance. When it is available to historians, it will occupy them for some time." But he increasingly suspected Heidemann's multiple stories about the diaries and their provenance. Despite the historian's own mounting skepticism, Rupert Murdoch rushed into print with the pithy comment, "Fuck Dacre. Publish."

Other historians in Germany and America were suspicious. Trevor-Roper reversed himself two days later, having become an object of mockery and satire in Great Britain. On Sunday, April 24, Trevor-Roper flew again to Hamburg and grilled Heidemann at great length on the diaries. Heidemann angrily accused the historian of behaving "exactly like an officer of the British army" in 1945—which Trevor-Roper had indeed been when he worked for British intelligence.

The following day Trevor-Roper admitted at a crowded press conference that "the thing looks more shaky" and the diaries could well be "a perfect forgery." In fact, on May 26, an East German forger and ex-convict named Konrad Kujau admitted in jail to West German police that he forged the entire set of diaries himself and that Heidemann knew all about it. The police promptly arrested Heidemann as a collaborator, and both men ended up serving jail terms for fraud.

Kujau had been collecting and forging Nazi memorabilia throughout the 1970s. Born in 1938, he was only seven at the end of the war. He embarked on a career as a locksmith, painter, construction worker, and waiter, all temporary jobs. In June 1957, he escaped East Germany and settled in West Berlin, then lived in a series of displaced persons camps and homeless shelters in West Germany. He bought and sold Nazi memorabilia, much of it fake. He was a compulsive liar and storyteller, much like Van Meegeren. He claimed that in 1970, Reinhard Gehlen of West German intelligence had given him forty pages of handwritten signatures to imitate to see if he would qualify as a forger. About 1980, using a published collection of Hitler's daily chronology, staining school notebooks with tea, and fastening the plastic initials "A.H." on

Illustration 2.3   **Konrad Kujau**

Konrad Kujau cheerfully forged the Hitler Diaries
but used paper and ink that were available only
after Hitler's death.

each cover, Kujau began producing the Hitler Diaries. On a good day,
he could crank out a notebook of Old High German script in Hitler's
handwriting in five hours.

Heidemann was Kujau's willing accomplice for many months.
Trevor-Roper was an easy mark. He had no time to examine the diaries,
compare their text with known sources, or discover their provenance. He
had spent his academic career assaulting and criticizing other historians
in print for their alleged mistakes and missteps. Now he was about to
get his justly deserved comeuppance.

In fairness, Heidemann had lied to Trevor-Roper and claimed that
the paper had been chemically analyzed and shown to be from the
1933–1945 period. Trevor-Roper believed him. "I was also impressed
by the sheer bulk of the diaries," the historian admitted. "Who, I asked
myself, would forge sixty volumes when six would have served his
purpose?" The answer was—Konrad Kujau.

Trevor-Roper, at the time almost seventy years old, should have known
better. With a brilliant record of scholarship at Christ Church College,
Oxford, the young historian had joined the Radio Security Services of
the British Secret Service (SIS, or MI6) in 1940 and been involved with

the decoding of Hitler's Ultra signals intercepts at Bletchley Park during the war. (In 1943 Stewart Menzies nearly fired Trevor-Roper for compromising Ultra by forwarding top-secret cipher traffic to an SIS officer in Moscow.) In 1945 he was tasked to investigate the circumstances of Hitler's death; the result was a best seller titled *The Last Days of Hitler* (1947). Thirty years later, Trevor-Roper researched and wrote a marvelous study of a British forger and con man, Edmund Backhouse, in his well-received *The Hermit of Peking* (1976). In 1979 Prime Minister Margaret Thatcher awarded him a life peerage as Baron Dacre of Glanton.

Despite his self-satisfied eminence, Trevor-Roper thoroughly disliked Germans and their language and culture. The "Hitler expert" of MI6 could neither read nor speak German very well. "I do not read German with great ease or pleasure," he once admitted. Trevor-Roper's superior intellect, sharp tongue, and snobbish ways made him many enemies along the way. Nevertheless, when his SIS superior Dick White asked him in September 1945 to dispel the rumors of Hitler's survival and flight to South America, Trevor-Roper interviewed Nazi leaders and produced a report within six weeks. In the postwar era, he edited selections of Hitler's "table talk," the letters of SS leader Martin Bormann, and the diaries of Joseph Goebbels. Trevor-Roper gladly accepted the role of expert on Hitler and the Nazis despite the fact that his real expertise lay in seventeenth-century British politics.

While Trevor-Roper pontificated and other historians argued, German and British forensics specialists quickly determined that the Hitler Diaries were bogus. Louis Ferdinand Werner, a state chemist for West German police headquarters in Wiesbaden, analyzed the paper, cover, bindings, and glue of one notebook and found that the paper was made after 1955. The bindings contained threads of polyamide fibers produced only after the war. Equally modern were the optical characteristics of the paper. Werner reported his results to Heidemann on March 28, 1983, well in advance of the publicity or publication of any diaries. The only problem was that Heidemann was in on the plot with Kujau and never told his superiors at *Stern*.

A British colleague of Trevor-Roper at MI6 confirmed the forgery. Julius Grant (1901–1991) was a chemist who worked for the John Dickinson Paper Company in the 1930s and was an expert on paper technology. During World War II, he helped MI6 produce forgery-proof ration books, edible paper for spies, and paper that retained invisible writing for use by British POWs. During the 1960s, Grant helped solve the "Great Train Robbery" case. He also showed that wartime dictator Benito Mussolini's supposed diaries were printed on paper made after 1956 (Mussolini died in 1944). As soon as Grant got hold of one of the Hitler Diaries, he fluoresced the paper under ultraviolet light and showed that the optical dyes were all of postwar origin.

Handwriting experts were also suspicious. Initially they found the handwriting convincing because they were given pages from different sections of the diaries to compare. Sure enough, Kujau's fake handwriting was consistent with Kujau's fake handwriting. Later they realized that the spacing between letters and words in the diaries was considerably larger than in Hitler's own hand.

The whole Hitler Diaries fiasco was a media circus brought on by Rupert Murdoch's lust for power and the supporting cast of journalists and historians eager to cash in on the publication of the diaries, forgery or not. Critics mocked Trevor-Roper as "Lord Lucre of Glenlivet" for his fees and his Scottish background. Forensics was a valuable tool, but most historians did not know enough to rely on that science. A few hours of forensic testing at the outset would have saved the journalists, the historians, and the police a lot of time and money. Indeed, the tests were carried out, and Gerd Heidemann was informed, but he did not tell anyone. Had he shared forensic knowledge, the worldwide sensation of the Hitler Diaries would never have made the front pages of the newspapers and an eminent historian would not have become a laughingstock for authenticating a forgery. Only after the media sensationalized the diaries did forensic science eliminate any claims to their authenticity. By then, real science was less interesting than fake documents, forensic history less interesting than Nazi mythology. For the media, the forensic facts simply got in the way of the story of the day.

2.4 Walter McCrone Again: Carbon-14 Dating the Shroud of Turin

No sooner had the Hitler Diaries affair subsided than Walter McCrone shifted his focus from the Vinland Map to the Shroud of Turin, in which Jesus supposedly was wrapped after his death on the cross. Discovered in the fourteenth century, the shroud had been a sacred relic of the Catholic Church for centuries. Critics had also been considering it a medieval painting, or forgery, since 1356. Finally, in April 1988, the Vatican approved a carbon-14 dating project to settle the issue.

According to legend, the Shroud of Turin was the linen cloth in which Jesus was buried after his crucifixion. A large sheet, thirteen feet long and three feet wide, the shroud displayed the distinct image of the face and body of a man. Supposedly the shroud traveled, shortly after Christ's death, from the Holy Land to Edessa, Syria, where it was venerated as the "Cloth of Edessa." In 943 the shroud was ransomed from Muslims and brought to Constantinople, the center of Eastern Christianity. It then disappeared from view when the Crusaders sacked Constantinople in 1204 and miraculously reappeared in a church in Lirey, France, in 1355. The shroud later moved to Chambéry, France, and in 1578 to Turin, Italy, where it became the property of the royal House of Savoy.

The shroud rarely appeared in public, notably at Napoleon's coronation in 1804 and then a decade later when the pope returned to Italy from a trip. There were shroud exhibits again in 1898 and 1931, then at an International Shroud Congress in 1950 in Rome. The debate as to whether the shroud was authentic or a fake continued until, in 1969, the Vatican decided to permit scientific testing of the shroud. Prior to 1973, there were no color photographs of the shroud, nor had it appeared on television.

In 1974 Father Peter Rinaldi approached Walter McCrone about testing and dating the shroud. Rinaldi had heard of McCrone's Chicago laboratory because of the Vinland Map controversy. The idea was to lift tiny samples from the shroud with a tungsten needle and examine them under a polarized light microscope. In addition, the Shroud of Turin Research Project (STURP), with which McCrone was at first associated, obtained thirty-two sticky tapes from different parts of the shroud, tapes that contained some 40,000 fibers.

By 1980 McCrone's team had discovered red ochre (iron oxide) particles on the tapes and was convinced that the shroud was a medieval painting from about 1355; using the Becke line test for refractive index, the team further showed that the linen exhibited no traces of blood. The scientists confirmed their light microscope results with a scanning electron microscope (SEM), published their results in 1981, and sent Vatican-approved scientists at STURP into an uproar. McCrone promptly resigned from STURP and worked on other projects.

In 1983 King Umberto II died and the Shroud of Turin passed to the ownership of the Catholic Church.

Shortly after the Hitler Diaries episode, both scientists and the Catholic Church began to consider dating the shroud using new carbon-14 dating techniques. Carbon-14 is the tiniest form of carbon found in

Illustration 2.4   **The Shroud of Turin**

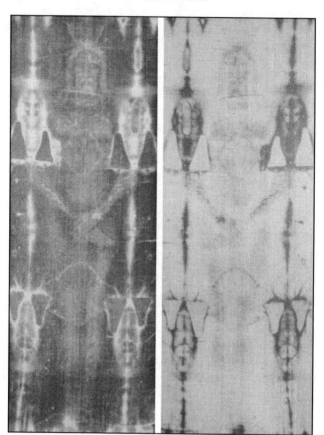

A negative and a photograph of a section of the Shroud of Turin.

nature and the only radioactive form. It has a half-life of 5,730 years. Only very small (50 mg) samples of the Shroud of Turin would be required for the experiment, using an accelerator mass spectrometry (AMS) apparatus.

In April 1988, the Vatican agreed to a carbon-dating experiment on the shroud under the supervision of the British Museum in London. Independent laboratories at Oxford University, the University of Arizona, the University of California-Berkeley, and the Zurich Institute for Middle Energy Physics would all receive samples for carbon-dating. The results were remarkably consistent, averaging 1325 plus or minus sixty-five years as the estimated date for the shroud, a range that easily included McCrone's earlier date of 1355.

On October 13, 1988, the Vatican announced that the Shroud of Turin was not an authentic relic because the carbon-dating experiments had placed it squarely in the fourteenth—not the first—century CE. Science and forensic history had trumped religion.

Two months later Helen Wallis, head of the Map Department at the British Museum, wrote Walter McCrone to thank him for his paper on the Vinland Map. "Which leads me on to the Turin Shroud," she wrote; "your results have been fully vindicated, as I expected."

The case of the Shroud of Turin showed how modern forensics techniques, again using analytical chemistry and mass spectrometry, could date fairly precisely any material object of which there was a sample available. For centuries, the shroud had been a venerated relic of the church. Critics had their suspicions, but no hard science to back them up. In the end, Walter McCrone was able to show that the reddish stains on the linen were red ochre paint, not blood, and that the linen itself dated from the fourteenth century. Case closed.

Except that in December 2011, Italian scientists claimed that the shroud could not have been a medieval forgery and that the marks on it were made by electromagnetic energy. Lasers were not around in the first century, so something miraculous must have happened. Forensic history had produced convincing evidence regarding the Shroud of Turin. And yet the debate goes on. Forensic history, like history, remains an argument without end.

2.5 Philippe Charlier: The Bogus Remains of Joan of Arc

Not all forgeries involve art works, maps, or documents. In 1867 a bottle supposedly containing the ashes of Joan of Arc turned up at a pharmacy in Paris labeled: "Remains found under the pyre of Joan of Arc, maiden of Orléans." In 2007 DNA analysis, microscopy, chemical analysis, and carbon dating by a young forensics scientist named Philippe Charlier showed that the bottle contained a human rib and a cat femur, some charcoal, and some textile scraps. Some were parts of Egyptian mummies common in medieval pharmaceuticals. Like the Shroud of Turin, the relics were fake.

Joan of Arc was the heroine of France, the Maid of Orléans, the teenager who fought against the English during the Hundred Years War and, in 1431, at the age of nineteen, was burned at the stake by the English as a witch. She was both a national legend in France and a martyr for the Catholic Church. The church beatified her in 1909 and then canonized her as a saint in 1920. During World War II, her symbolic Cross of Lorraine became the flag of the Free French movement in London exile and then of the movement's leader, Charles de Gaulle. De Gaulle once told U.S. president Franklin D. Roosevelt, "I am Joan of Arc." Roosevelt was both amused and annoyed at the egomania of his difficult wartime ally.

Relics and legends of Joan of Arc abounded, especially in the Normandy area where she lived and fought. In 1867 a Paris pharmacist claimed to have a set of relics found in the cathedral town of Rouen—a human rib, blackened wood, a small piece of linen, and the thigh-bone or femur of a cat. Presumably the human rib belonged to Joan, the blackened wood came from the fiery stake on which she perished in flames, the linen was from her dress, and the cat femur testified to the medieval practice of throwing in a feline sacrifice when a witch was burned at the stake. The relics were duly venerated and ultimately moved to a museum in Chinon near Tours.

But were the relics authentic? Forensic scientists and historians decided to try to find out.

In 2006 a medical assistant at Raymond Poincaré Hospital in the suburb of Garches outside Paris came across the Joan relics and decided to test them with the tools of modern forensic science. Philippe Charlier, a forensic anthropologist, dutifully obtained permission from the Catholic Church to proceed. He then utilized spectrometry, an electron microscope, pollen analysis, and carbon-14 tests for his experiments.

Charlier discovered that the bones dated from the seventh to third century BCE, not the fifteenth century or 1867, and were most probably from an Egyptian mummy. The black crust on everything was not from the charred remains of a fire, but from an embalming mix of wood resin, bitumen, and malachite. The linen also turned out to be from a mummy wrapping. The relics of Joan of Arc were cobbled together from the mummified remains of an ancient Egyptian tomb—common enough in Europe during and after the Middle Ages.

Who forged the relics? We don't know. Perhaps the entrepreneurial pharmacist was the culprit. Perhaps he was not. Perhaps a fan of Joan sought to support the campaign to make her a saint. No one confessed to the crime. There was no provenance for the relics. Forensic science could only take us so far. In this case, Charlier proved that the relics were not

Illustration 2.5 **Joan of Arc**

The purported remains of the Maid of Orléans proved to be fake, but this 1879 painting by Jules Bastien-Lepage shows the power of her cult.

authentic by dating them and examining the components of the materials. He figured out how a forgery was done, but not "whodunit" or even when it was done. He could date the materials, but not the forgery.

Forensics is a powerful modern tool in determining the authenticity of artifacts and art objects. The forensic historian can use science to date such materials and establish whether they were created at a particular time or not. Forgery is a crime susceptible to the analysis of forensics. So is murder. In the case of some famous homicides, forensics provides some tantalizing and even convincing evidence, but not enough to close off debate.

References

2.1 The three major sources on chemist Paul Coremans and the forger Han Van Meegeren are Edward Dolnick, *The Forger's Spell* (New York: HarperCollins, 2008); Jonathan Lopez, *The Man Who Made Vermeers* (New York: Houghton Mifflin, 2009); and Paul Coremans, *Van Meegeren's Faked Vermeers and de Hooghs: A Scientific Examination* (Amsterdam: J.M. Meulenhoff, 1949).

2.2 On Walter McCrone and the Vinland Map: The "official" Yale version of the map's history is by R.A. Skelton, Thomas E. Marston, and George D. Painter, *The Vinland Map and the Tatar Relation* (New Haven, CT: Yale University Press, 1995). The best scholarly account is by Kirsten A. Seaver, *Maps, Myths, and Men: The Story of the Vinland Map* (Stanford, CA: Stanford University Press, 2004).

2.3 Julius Grant's work on the Hitler Diaries is described in Charles Hamilton, *The Hitler Diaries: Fakes That Fooled the World* (Lexington: University Press of Kentucky, 1991), and Robert Harris, *Selling Hitler* (New York: Pantheon, 1986). The best account of Hugh Trevor-Roper's involvement in the case is Adam Sisman, *An Honorable Englishman: The Life of Hugh Trevor-Roper* (New York: Random House, 2010), 510–539.

2.4 Evidence on Walter McCrone and the Shroud of Turin comes from Walter McCrone, *Judgment Day for the Shroud of Turin* (Amherst, NY: Prometheus Books, 1999), and Leoncio A. Garza-Valdes, *The DNA of God? Newly Discovered Secrets of the Shroud of Turin* (New York: Berkley Books, 1999). A more recent work is by Robert K. Wilcox, *The Truth About the Shroud of Turin: Solving the Mystery* (Washington, DC: Regnery, 2010).

2.5 On Philippe Charlier's investigation of the alleged relics of Joan of Arc, see the British Broadcasting Corporation's intriguing report issued on April 4, 2007, at http://news.bbc.co.uk/go/pr/fr/-/2/hi/science/nature/6527105.stm.

Atomic Evidence

Atomic evidence refers to evidence produced when a beam of neutrons from a nuclear reactor bombards hair, bones, bullets, or any other substance and then identifies components of that substance by measuring emitted radiation. Atomic evidence—in the form of neutron activation analysis, or NAA—was discovered in 1937 but was not widely used until the 1950s, when access to nuclear reactors became possible. NAA evidence first helped convict a criminal in court in 1958 when a Madawaska, Maine, man, John Vollman, murdered his Canadian girlfriend and the ratio of sulfur radiation to phosphorus in hair clutched in her hand was found to resemble his hair more than hers.

In 1960 the age of nuclear power was in its infancy. The first reactors were going online and producing electricity. Reactors also served as powerful new research tools in medicine and forensics, especially valuable as a source of neutrons that could analyze material evidence. Such analysis confirmed the presence of substantial amounts of arsenic in Napoleon's hair, but did not resolve the question of whether he was murdered by a royalist aide during his exile on the island of St. Helena.

John F. Kennedy was elected U.S. president in 1960 and assassinated in Dallas three years later. Whether he was murdered by a lone gunman or by a conspiracy was (and is) the subject of enormous debate. Only in 1977 were the bullets from Lee Harvey Oswald's rifle analyzed professionally using NAA, although the FBI had attempted its first NAA in 1964. More than a decade later, a similar analysis at Oak Ridge National Laboratory in Tennessee suggested that another U.S. president, Zachary Taylor, did not exhibit sufficient arsenic in his body to justify a claim of murder.

Nobody suggested that the composer Ludwig von Beethoven was murdered, but in 2000 scientists did observe evidence of lead poisoning in his hair samples. Once again, neutron activation analysis enabled historians to make a more accurate judgment regarding the causes of Beethoven's death. Atomic evidence can at times be a form of historical evidence and thus subject to the same arguments and cross-examination about whether historical claims are true or false.

Sten Forshufvud: The Arsenic in Napoleon's Hair

In 1955 Sten Forshufvud (1903–1955), a Swedish dental surgeon, read the newly published memoirs of Louis Marchand, Napoleon's valet during his final exile on the island of St. Helena, and became convinced that the emperor had died of arsenic poisoning. In time, Forshufvud came to believe that Napoleon had been murdered and used NAA tests to try to prove the emperor's death a homicide.

Dentists and odontologists work on teeth. But Forshufvud wanted to run tests on Napoleon's hair. To do this he needed to get access to a nuclear reactor, not an easy task in 1960.

In the beginning, the usual historical, but not forensic, evidence sparked the Swedish odontologist's interest. Marchand's memoirs specified thirty-one symptoms of poor health, including weakness, stomach pains, and vomiting, during Napoleon's last days when he lived under house arrest at the Longwood estate on St. Helena. Forshufvud concluded that twenty-eight of the symptoms suggested arsenic poisoning. Had Napoleon been murdered?

Forshufvud had studied biology at Lund University and dentistry at the University of Bordeaux in France, then bacteriology and pathology at Goteberg. He was much more than a dentist. He held the prestigious post of professor of odontology at the Nobel Institute of Physics in Stockholm, and he read widely in the literature on serology, plasma, and poisons. In 1959 he read an article by Hamilton Smith of the Department of Forensic Medicine at the University of Glasgow in Scotland and decided to request that Smith bombard samples of Napoleon's hair with neutrons to determine the arsenic levels. A few months later, Forshufvud obtained hair samples—allegedly Napoleon's—from an assistant curator of the Malmaison Museum in France, Henry Lachouque. Forshufvud then sent them off to Glasgow for testing without identifying their famous owner to the scientist who was testing them.

Illustration 3.1   **Napoleon on St. Helena**

Sten Forshufvud, a Swedish odontologist, thought that Napoleon had been murdered in 1821 by one of his trusted aides using arsenic. But was it true?

The postmortem report by British medical officers on May 6, 1821, had concluded that Napoleon died from extensive cancerous lesions of the stomach. Napoleon's household physician, Francesco Antommarchi, performed an autopsy on Napoleon's body and concluded to the contrary that Napoleon died from hepatitis, not stomach cancer. But Napoleon himself had written in several places that he thought the British were arranging to have him murdered.

The poison of choice in those days was white arsenic, known as arsenious oxide or arsenic trioxide, or As_2O_3, an odorless and untraceable compound. Only in 1836 did James Marsh, a British chemist at the Royal Arsenal in Woolwich, develop a test for arsenic. Body fluid or tissue added to a glass vessel with zinc and acid would produce an arsine gas, IFF, when arsenic was present. The test was quickly applied in France to prove in a court of law that a deceased French foundry owner's wife had poisoned him.

Four years later, in 1840, Napoleon's body was exhumed and brought to Paris for reburial. The body was extremely well preserved, common enough in the presence of arsenic.

In 1960 a Napoleonic hair sample was ideal for testing. Hair grows out of a tiny follicle attached to the skin by a root bulb. Each hair has three layers—medulla, cortex, and cuticle—and grows at a rate of about one centimeter each month. Forensic scientists normally cut hair samples into one-centimeter lengths for analysis.

Neutron activation analysis around 1960 was cumbersome and required access to a nuclear reactor that could produce a neutron beam. Neutrons that were fired at a sample material caused that sample to emit radiation in the form of gamma rays. Emitted radiation levels revealed the chemical makeup of the material. The process was especially useful in analyzing hair, paint, soil, and metal (e.g., bullets).

On June 22, 1960, Forshufvud mailed the hair samples to Professor Hamilton Smith in Glasgow, not mentioning Napoleon by name. He asked simply: Is arsenic to be found? He also asked two further questions: Did the hair samples belong to the same person? Did the samples contain antinomy and mercury as well as arsenic?

To answer these questions, Smith turned to experts at Harwell, Britain's top-secret nuclear weapons facility. The hair was irradiated with thermal neutrons and tested for arsenic. The test results showed that there was "exposure to large amounts of arsenic," namely, 10.38 and 10.53 ppm as opposed to a normal expected reading of 0.86 ppm. Napoleon's arsenic levels exceeded ten times the norm. Smith reported these results (again, by regular mail) to Forshufvud. There was no charge for the work.

A year later, Smith and Forshufvud published their results in *Nature* in an article titled "Arsenic Content of Napoleon I's Hair Probably Taken Immediately after His Death." They concluded that Napoleon died of "chronic and acute types of arsenic poisoning." A few months later, they published another article in the same journal concluding that Napoleon was "exposed to arsenic intermittently over time." By this they meant that regular prescribed doses of calomel combined with orgeat, with its bitter almond taste, would have gradually released mercury salts (mercurious cyanide) that were both poisonous and corrosive to the stomach lining.

By 1964 Smith had conducted some 140 tests on Napoleon's hair samples that led to the same conclusions. Forshufvud trumpeted his murder-by-arsenic theory in a 1961 book published in London and wickedly titled *Who Killed Napoleon?* He then made contact with a Canadian businessman and body builder named Ben Weider, an amateur

Napoleon buff, who later coauthored books with the Swedish dentist titled *Assassination on St. Helena* (1978) and *The Murder of Napoleon* (1982). After Forshufvud died in 1983, Weider reissued the work as *Assassination at St. Helena Revisited* in 1995. By this time the two men had concluded that the culprit was Charles Tristan, Marquis de Montholon, a royalist enemy of Napoleon within his own household on St. Helena who had both opportunity and motive to kill the emperor. But did he really commit murder?

But there is one more thing, as Lt. Columbo used to say on television. In 1982 David E.H. Jones published another article in *Nature* arguing that Napoleon could well have been poisoned by years of exposure to the wallpaper in the house at Longwood. Arsenic was in common use at the time in fashion, perfume, tapestry, food preservation, and, yes indeed, wallpaper. The green pigment in the wallpaper at Longwood contained arsenic. Mold broke down the arsenic gradually over time into toxic dimethyl and trimethyl arsine, dangerous to inhale and potentially fatal. But if the wallpaper were the culprit, why were other residents of Longwood not affected by exposure?

In 2005 Swiss researchers in Basle and Zurich measured more than a dozen pairs of pants that Napoleon wore during his last two decades of his life. The man who weighed 148 pounds in 1800 had ballooned to 200 pounds by 1820, then dropped down to 174 pounds at the end of his life. The weight gain and loss pattern was quite consistent with a controlled sample of 270 male patients who suffered from stomach cancer, the medical diagnosis by Napoleon's doctors after they autopsied his body.

But a year later toxicologists again sampled Napoleon's hair, this time with a new ICP-MS (inductively coupled plasma-mass spectrometry) machine and discovered again "massive amounts" of arsenic and antinomy along with "elevated levels" of mercury and lead. The arsenic levels in Napoleon's hair were now forty times the expected normal level for someone living at that time.

In August 2007, the Forensic Science Institute again discovered large amounts of arsenic in Napoleon's hair. Mass spectrometry used in toxicology to test for heavy metal poisoning showed that over 97 percent of the arsenic was inorganic, not organic. This result was consistent with "chronic intoxication." The arsenic poisoning theory seemed alive and well.

Finally, in 2008, a team of ten scientists at Italy's National Institute of Nuclear Physics in Milan-Bicocca and Pavia analyzed hair from four different periods in Napoleon's life: when he was a boy in Corsica; when he was living in exile on Elba; on the day he died in 1821; and on the day after his death. Hair samples came from four different museums and were tested by NAA in a nuclear reactor at Pavia. But this time, scientists found no rise in arsenic levels in Napoleon's hair at all. In addition, they also found high levels of arsenic in the hair samples of his wife Josephine and his son Napoleon II. In fact, all three individuals showed arsenic levels nearly 100 times the norm.

After fifty years, forensic scientists and historians have discovered and interpreted a great deal of evidence bearing on the issue of Napoleon's death, but have not proved that he was—or was not—murdered. The high levels of arsenic measured were consistent with those of other family members and with common environmental exposure to arsenic. Nuclear activation analysis produced accurate and consistent results on the toxicology of Napoleon's hair. But only further forensic historical investigation and evidence will be able to tell us exactly how Napoleon died.

Just to make things interesting, in 2011 a British expert on Jane Austen suggested that the great writer herself might also have been murdered with arsenic in 1817, four years before Napoleon's death. Indeed, until the Marsh test, arsenic was the untraceable weapon of choice for culprits wanting to poison someone. But was it really murder, she wrote? Who knows!

In any event, arsenic was ubiquitous in the early nineteenth century, a toxic component used in many household places, from the bathroom to the dining room. Too much exposure to arsenic could kill you. It may have killed Napoleon.

3.2 Vincent Guinn: The "Magic Bullet" and the Kennedy Assassination

In 1977 nuclear chemist Vincent Guinn applied neutron activation analysis (NAA) to one of the most traumatic and hotly debated historical events of our time, the assassination of U.S. president John F. Kennedy. In so doing, Guinn became a forensic historian and expert witness in court.

On November 22, 1963, Kennedy was shot and killed while riding in a limousine in Dealey Plaza in Dallas, Texas; Texas governor John Connally was wounded. The Warren Commission, established by President

Lyndon Johnson (named after its chair, Supreme Court justice Earl Warren), concluded in 1964 that the killer was a lone gunman, Lee Harvey Oswald, firing from the Texas School Book Depository. Oswald denied killing anybody and said he was a "patsy." But Oswald was killed the next day and no trial was held.

In 1977 Vincent Guinn conducted neutron activation tests on bullet fragments and found that they all came from two bullets fired by Oswald's rifle. Modern ballistics tests and autopsy photographs have convinced a minority that a second "head shot" bullet from a grassy knoll killed Kennedy, implying a conspiracy, perhaps involving the Dallas Mafia. But no other bullets or bullet fragments have been found. Despite forensic evidence, the case cannot be considered closed and the historical debate goes on: lone gunman or conspiracy?

Among the early conspiracy theorists in 1964 who read and rejected the Warren Commission conclusions was none other than Hugh Trevor-Roper, the British historian who jumped to conclusions without evidence two decades later when he authenticated the bogus Hitler Diaries. Over the years conspiracy theories abounded, in part because the Dallas police never sealed off any of the crime scenes from curious bystanders and souvenir seekers. This heightened suspicions that evidence was removed, altered, or disposed of improperly.

According to the Warren Commission, only three bullets were fired at Kennedy. One missed. The second entered the president's neck at a downward angle of 25 degrees, passed through his neck, and then passed through Connally's neck and right armpit, exiting below the right nipple and passing through his right wrist and then his left thigh, leaving tiny fragments. The third shot hit Kennedy in the head, causing massive brain damage and a fatal wound. The second bullet was found on a stretcher used by Connally at Parkland Hospital, Trauma Room 2. Because of its unusual trajectory, course, and damage, it became known as the "magic bullet," or Commission Exhibit CE 399.

In 1964 the Warren Commission asked the FBI to analyze all the bullets and bullet fragments found in Dallas. These included two copper-jacketed bullets recovered from Connally's hospital stretcher and two large fragments found in the president's limousine, all fired from Oswald's 1940 6.5 mm Mannichler-Carcano rifle. The FBI concluded that Oswald fired three shots. One shot missed, the second passed through Kennedy's back and throat, the third shot entered his head. But the results were inconclusive.

Illustration 3.2   **The "Magic Bullet"**

CE 399, the "magic bullet" that passed through President Kennedy and Texas governor John Connally in Dallas on November 22, 1963.

But in 1964 the FBI's emission spectroscopy tests, the FBI's first use of NAA (at Oak Ridge National Laboratory), were both novel and questionable. The FBI was inexperienced in this area of forensics. It had never made use of NAA before and had difficulty interpreting the results of the tests. The tests were, in any event, conducted in secret, and the American public remained highly skeptical of the Warren Commission report and of any new statements regarding the assassination that came from the U.S. government, especially in the wake of the 1968 assassinations of the president's brother, Senator Robert Kennedy, and the civil rights leader Martin Luther King.

Until the 1970s, people did not even know that the FBI had conducted NAA tests on the Kennedy assassination bullets and bullet fragments. Then, in 1977, the House Select Committee on Assassinations (HSCA) began to assemble a team of forensic specialists to reexamine the evidence from the murders of John Kennedy, Robert Kennedy, and Martin Luther King. The

Table 3.1

The Bullet Fragments

Specimen	Description	Weight (grains)
CE 399 (Q1)	Bullet from stretcher	158.6
CE 567 (Q2)	Bullet fragment from seat cushion next to driver	44.6
CE 569 (Q3)	Bullet fragment from floor to right of front seat	21.0
CE 843 (Q4)	Metal fragment from the president's head	1.65
CE 843 (Q5)	Metal fragment from the president's head	0.15
CE 842 (Q9)	Metal fragment from the arm of Governor Connally	0.5
CE 840 (Q14)	Three metal fragments removed from rear floorboard carpet	0.9; 0.7; 0.7
CE 841 (Q15)	Scraping from inside surface of windshield	None listed

Note: List of bullets and fragments received by the FBI and analyzed by emission spectroscopy and neutron activation analysis (www.karws.gso.uri.edu/jfk/jfk.html, Table 11).

scientists had first begun to organize in 1972 as the Physical Anthropology Section within the American Academy of Forensic Sciences. Among the fourteen charter members were chemist Walter McCrone, forensic anthropologist Clyde Snow, New York City chief medical examiner and pathologist Michael Baden, odontologist Lowell Levine, anthropologist Ellis Kerley, and Vincent Guinn. The HSCA hired all of them as consultants or contractors to help analyze evidence from the assassinations. Baden headed the all-star forensic team and helped pick its members, many of whom would go on to investigate other cases of forensic history.

Vincent Perrie Guinn (1917–2002) was professor of radiochemistry at the University of California, Irvine, and one of the world's leading experts on NAA. After receiving BS and MS degrees in chemistry from the University of Southern California shortly before World War II, Guinn completed his PhD in 1949 at Harvard University under George Kistiakovsky, a world-renowned chemist who worked at Los Alamos on the Manhattan Project to build an atomic bomb during the war. During the 1950s Guinn studied radiochemistry at the Oak Ridge Institute of Nuclear Studies before becoming head of the Shell Development Company's Radiochemistry Group in California. In 1961 he moved to

San Diego to work on NAA in the General Atomic Division of General Dynamics. Guinn was one of the first scientists to recognize the applications of NAA to forensics.

In 1969 Guinn joined the chemistry faculty at the University of California, Irvine, where he taught until his retirement in 1988. In addition to his teaching and research, Guinn appeared as an expert witness in more than 150 court cases and became an expert on gunshot residue analysis. In 1979 Guinn won the prestigious George Hevesy Medal for his work on NAA. He was also an avid hiker and athlete who loved entertaining people. In 1986 he cheerfully appeared in the British film *On Trial, Lee Harvey Oswald*, playing himself testifying before HSCA. In November 2003, shortly after his death, Guinn's testimony appeared on Court TV.

Vincent Guinn was ideally qualified to analyze the bullets and bullet fragments from Oswald's rifle, a 5.6 mm Mannlicher-Carcano M91 bolt-action rifle with a side-mounted Ordnance Optics 4x18 scope. The 1940 Italian-made rifle fired full-metal-jacket bullets at a muzzle velocity of over 2,000 feet per second. In September 1977, the HSCA arranged for bullets and bullet fragments—the same ones examined by the FBI in 1964—to be taken to Guinn's California laboratory for NAA testing at the university research reactor.

In mid-September, a courier from the National Archives, James L. Gear, left Washington, DC, accompanied by two federal guards and flew to California. Here Guinn had three days to examine the bullet specimens for trace elements produced by a neutron beam. Samples were placed in a polyethylene vial, introduced into the reactor, and bombarded with neutrons until the samples became radioactive. Scientists could then measure the rates of radioactive decay, or half-lives, of the three elements common in bullets—antimony, silver, and copper. New gamma ray detectors then recorded their emissions.

Mannlicher-Carcano ammunition was unusual. The last batch manufactured for rifles—over a million rounds—was made in 1954 by the Western Cartridge Company in East Alton, Illinois. Guinn received the bullets from a forensic pathologist at the University of Kansas, John Nichols. In 1974 Nichols finally succeeded in obtaining a copy of the FBI's 1964 file on its NAA testing of the assassination bullets. Nichols and Guinn soon discovered that all Mannlicher-Carcano bullets exhibited lower antimony levels than most ammunition and that there was no uniformity in their distribution, from bullet to bullet or even within the same bullet. Mannlicher-Carcano bullets were unique in their lack of uniformity.

Like the FBI in 1964, Guinn tested bullet fragments found in the presidential limousine, fragments taken from Governor Connally's wrist, and the "magic bullet" found on the stretcher at Parkland Hospital. He compared these with samples from the 1954 batch of Mannlicher-Carcano ammunition. The two Kennedy bullets and the ammunition matched perfectly.

Guinn's results provided support for the single-bullet theory by showing that the "magic bullet" recovered on the stretcher (CE 399) was indistinguishable in its antinomy concentrations from the metal fragment taken from Connally's wrist (CE 842). His results also were consistent with the FBI results of 1964.

In his testimony before the HSCA, Guinn cited evidence that there were two, and only two, bullets in the specimens examined. He went on to say that "those two specimens, CE 399 and 842 agree so closely in their antimony concentration that I could not distinguish one from the other." Guinn's conclusion seemed to support both the Warren Commission report and the 1964 FBI NAA report.

The HSCA in the end concluded that Lee Harvey Oswald had indeed shot and killed President Kennedy from his nest in the Texas School Book Depository, but added that a second shooter and a conspiracy to kill the president were "probable." However, there was no ballistic evidence to support this claim.

So the debate goes on. In 1981 British writer Michael Eddowes succeeded in having Lee Harvey Oswald's body exhumed to test his theory that Oswald was really the double of a Soviet assassin. But dental records and a mastoid scar proved that Oswald was in fact Oswald. In 1993 Gerald Posner in his book *Case Closed* described Vincent Guinn's tests as confirming that only two bullets, both from Oswald's rifle, had killed Kennedy and wounded Connally. Guinn's results effectively ended speculation that someone had planted the "magic bullet" on the stretcher or that there were more bullets involved.

Yet in 2010 a book by G. Paul Chambers titled *Head Shot: The Science behind the JFK Assassination* does not even mention Guinn or his test results, even though the book emphasizes ballistics. Contradicting Guinn's results, which are inconvenient for his theory, Chambers argues that there was a second shooter.

The historical debate over the Kennedy assassination is likely to continue indefinitely. No additional bullets have been found to prove that a second shooter fired at Kennedy in Dallas. The Guinn NAA analysis strongly suggests that Oswald killed the president with two bullets, but does not bear on the question of whether or not the Mafia, a secret government agency, or Cuban leader Fidel Castro might have been involved in a conspiracy to kill him. Certainly the Texas and Louisiana Mafias had ample reason to wish to stop the Kennedy brothers' war on crime. They said so on many occasions. Conspiracy theories of history tend to flourish without reference to forensic evidence, which often suggests that no conspiracy is required to explain why and how a crime was committed. Forensic historians, of course, will continue their argument without end. And the media will stand ready to accept any new and plausible theory regarding the murder of President Kennedy, at least until the public loses interest.

3.3 William Maples: The Death of Zachary Taylor

In 1991 a novelist named Clara Rising persuaded the descendants of the twelfth U.S. president, Zachary Taylor (1784–1850), to permit the exhumation of his body. Taylor had died under strange circumstances in the summer of 1850. There were subsequent rumors that proslavery conspirators had poisoned the president because of his opposition to extending slavery into the territories. Neutron activation analysis of Taylor's hair and nails at the Oak Ridge National Laboratory showed that he had arsenic levels far below those that might have suggested he was poisoned. Case closed, it would seem.

Historians agreed that President Zachary Taylor, nicknamed "Old Rough and Ready" because of his Mexican War exploits, had died on July 9, 1850, of gastroenteritis. The summer in Washington, DC, was typically sweltering. On the Fourth of July, Taylor had consumed a large meal of raw vegetables, fresh cherries, and iced buttermilk after helping break ground for the new Washington Monument. Shortly thereafter an acute case of diarrhea forced him to take to his bed. Within a few days he was dead at the age of sixty-six, only sixteen months into his presidency. Had the president of the United States ended his days with a bad case of indigestion on a sweltering Independence Day in the nation's capital? Or had he been murdered?

In 1991, Clara Rising, a writer with a PhD in English from the University of Florida, published a historical novel on the Civil War titled *Season of the Wild Rose*. In the process of researching and writing the novel, Rising became convinced that Zachary Taylor might well have

Illustration 3.3   **Zachary Taylor**

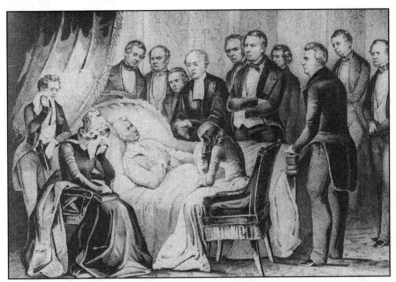

Was President Zachary Taylor, seen here on his deathbed, a victim of gastroenteritis or murder?

been poisoned. She was then working on a book about Taylor and had discovered that his symptoms at the end included vomiting, diarrhea, abdominal spasms, and weakness. Persistent and single-minded, she approached William Maples, a forensic anthropologist and professor at the University of Florida in Gainesville. Maples was not immediately enthusiastic when Rising mentioned the possibility of exhuming Taylor's body and testing it for traces of arsenic poisoning. He pointed out that the remains of the dead belong legally to the family, not to the cemeteries that house the body. Sure enough, with her usual persistence Rising received family permission to exhume the body at the Zachary Taylor National Cemetery in Louisville, Kentucky. Maples then agreed to help.

William Maples (1937–1997) was born in Dallas and attended the University of Texas at Austin before receiving his PhD in anthropology in 1967. Maples had become fascinated with forensic anthropology as a boy when a deputy sheriff showed him autopsy photographs of the notorious bank robbers Bonnie Parker and Clyde Barrow. After getting married and doing field research in Kenya in the 1960s, Maples went to the University of Florida in Gainesville as assistant professor of anthropology. He remained there until his death, also serving as a consultant to the New York State Police (where he became acquainted with odontologist Lowell Levine and medical examiner Michael Baden) and to the U.S. Army Central Identification Laboratory in Honolulu (where Mildred Trotter had done her research on long bones).

Maples worked on a number of important forensic cases involving historical figures. In 1984 he went to Lima, Peru, examined bones in the cathedral crypt, and confirmed that they belonged to the famous Spanish explorer Pizarro. The body showed evidence of multiple stab wounds and was missing hands and genitals. The evidence amply supported the known historical fact that assassins murdered Pizarro while he was attending mass on June 25, 1541. But Maples discovered that the mummy inside the glass-walled sarcophagus in the cathedral chapel was not in fact Pizarro, as advertised, but an impostor, who was duly replaced by the real Pizarro skeleton from the cathedral crypt.

In addition, Betty Pat Gatliff of SKULLpture Inc., an Oklahoma firm that specialized in facial reconstruction along the lines of Gerasimov's work in the Soviet Union, was able to create a clay bust of Pizarro from the bones and skull. The bust was gratefully accepted as a gift by a convent in Pizarro's hometown of Trujillo, Spain. No one could prove, of course, how accurate the facial reconstruction of Pizarro, a rough contemporary of Gerasimov's subject, Ivan the Terrible, was.

In 1992 Maples became involved in examining bones exhumed in Siberia and confirming that they were indeed the bones of the family of the last Romanov tsar, Nicholas II. But in between Pizarro and the Romanovs, Maples had to figure out whether or not Zachary Taylor had been murdered.

On June 27, 1991, Maples was present when the body of Taylor was removed from his crypt for five hours and examined by the local coroner, Dr. Richard Greathouse, aided by the Kentucky state medical examiner George Nichols II. Thanks to advanced publicity, the exhumation of a U.S. president became a media circus complete with rolling TV cameras, trucks with satellite dishes, reporters, and a large crowd of bystanders. The story was all over CNN, *Good Morning America*, and the *Today* show. Taylor's lead-lined casket was moved to the medical examiner's office. Because Taylor's body had been originally placed on ice and not embalmed, there were none of the usual traces of arsenic from the embalming process, only a macabre-looking skeleton in formal funeral attire.

The analysts took photographs of Taylor's body. An odontologist examined Taylor's teeth. Samples of hair, nails, clothing, and bone were removed. The body was then returned to its crypt and resting place. Two identical sets of the samples were sent off to laboratories—the Kentucky state toxicology lab in Lexington and the Oak Ridge National Laboratory near Knoxville—where NAA tests confirmed that arsenic levels were normal for anyone living in the early to mid-nineteenth century. At Oak Ridge, two scientists, Larry Robinson and Frank Dyer of the chemical and analytical sciences division, working late into the evening, directed a beam of neutrons from the high flux isotope reactor onto the samples and then measured the energy levels for arsenic in the emitted gamma rays. By the time he returned to Gainesville, Maples knew the results. The arsenic levels were normal for anyone buried in a crypt for 141 years. "He was not poisoned," concluded George Nichols. In short order, the case of Zachary Taylor was closed and the public lost interest.

But the historical fact remained that Taylor in 1850 opposed the extension of slavery to the territories petitioning to become states, such as California and New Mexico, and had many enemies among slave-holders in the South. Clara Rising admitted that "we found the truth" using forensics and NAA, but that even so Taylor's "political enemies benefitted from his removal, whether they removed him or not." Rising at least deserved credit for persuading Taylor's descendants to permit exhumation and thus forensic tests.

Still, in 1999, Michael Parenti in his book *History as Mystery* asserted that historical conventional wisdom had trumped empirical forensic science. Six weeks after George Nichols announced that Taylor had died a "natural" death and had not been poisoned by arsenic, there was still no written medical report available. The brief summary released was three pages long, double-spaced, and was undated and unsigned by anyone. Yet the summary admitted that Taylor's symptoms were "clearly consistent with arsenic poisoning." Huh?

The average arsenic concentration in people is 0.2 to .06 ppm. Michael Ward of the Kentucky Department of Health Services, using colorimetric spectrophotometry, found up to 1.9 ppm in Taylor's hair, three to nine times the norm. His nails revealed 3.0 ppm, five to fifteen times the norm. Parenti noted that Sten Forshufvud and Hamilton Smith, analysts of Napoleon's hair, had distinguished between whole-hair and hair-root samples. Kennedy assassination ballistics expert Vincent Guinn, now at the University of Maryland, told Parenti that hair-root samples could have up to ten times as much arsenic concentration as whole-hair samples. Frank Dyer at Oak Ridge told Parenti that he had spoken with Nichols, who did not understand that the root ends should be measured. Dyer also informed Nichols that he found poisonous concentrations of antimony up to 10.0 ppm in Taylor's root hairs. Nichols never called Dyer to clarify the results, and never reported the high antinomy levels in his brief report.

So apparently the presence of high arsenic levels was never explained by the authorities, and the high antinomy levels never got reported. The Taylor case was at least open, not closed.

Clara Rising agreed. She pursued her case in *The Taylor File: The Mysterious Death of a President* (2007). In the Zachary Taylor case, forensics apparently trumped conspiracy theory. But perhaps the conventional wisdom of history in the Old South had trumped forensics by ignoring it. Old Rough and Ready had indeed died of gastroenteritis, known as cholera morbus in those days. But why? Was this "natural"? Perhaps his doctors killed him with doses of ipecac, calomel, opium, and quinine as they bled and blistered him. A few historians speculated that the doctors might have been in league with southern slaveholders. Only further historical evidence and research, not necessarily forensics, will come closer to an answer to such historical questions and speculations. But the forensics results of 1991 were incomplete, unreported, or suppressed, so the historical debate must continue.

3.4 William Walsh: Testing Beethoven's Hair

Samples of Ludwig van Beethoven's hair were treasured mementos in Europe after the composer's death in 1827. In 2000 William Walsh, a chemical engineer and expert on hair analysis, tested hair samples at Argonne National Laboratories using an APS (advanced photon source) machine and found above-average levels of lead, suggesting the cause of Beethoven's many maladies toward the end of his life. Tests in 2005 confirmed high lead levels, but then a New York lead poisoning expert examined two skull fragments in 2010 and found normal levels. Beethoven may not have been murdered, but he may well have died of lead poisoning.

In December 1994, the London auction house of Sotheby's sold a lock of Beethoven's hair designated H151492 to an unidentified American buyer for £3,600, or about $5,000. Cut from Beethoven's head after he died on March 27, 1827, the hair actually went to two buyers, not one: Ira Brilliant, a retired real estate developer in Phoenix, Arizona, and Alfredo ("Che") Guevara, a Mexican-American physician and urologist. At a press conference in Tucson a year later (December 1995), the two owners revealed that the lock of hair, which had passed through the hands of a Danish family that sheltered Jews during World War II, would now be divided (by legal contract), with 73 percent of the hair going to Ira Brilliant's Center for Beethoven Studies in San Jose, California, and 27 percent going to Guevara for scientific testing of chemical content.

Ira Brilliant had been collecting Beethoven artifacts since the 1970s. Brilliant's father, a Russian Jew, had moved to the United States before World War I. Brilliant himself had been a chemical warfare specialist in the U.S. Army during World War II, made a significant amount of money in real estate, and then began collecting first editions of Beethoven's music scores. By 1983 he owned seventy of them. Alfredo Guevara had grown up in Nogales, Texas, and attended Northwestern University in Chicago, where his roommate quite naturally nicknamed him "Che" after the Cuban revolutionary. Brilliant and Guevara met in Arizona in the 1990s and became friends with a common passion for Beethoven artifacts and music.

Once they had acquired the lock of Beethoven's hair, the two men hired forensic anthropologist Walter Birkby to examine the strands under a microscope. Birkby, a U.S. Marine veteran of the Korean War, taught forensic anthropology and pathology at the University of Arizona while consulting for the Pima County Office of the Medical Examiner. (Students facetiously called Birkby's laboratory "Birkby's Body Shoppe.") Birkby discovered that there were follicles at the roots of individual Beethoven hairs, so that DNA testing was feasible. There turned out to be 582 hairs in the Beethoven sample, so that by the terms of their contract 422 hairs would go to Brilliant's Center for Beethoven Studies and the 160 hairs belonging to Guevara would be tested in a laboratory.

Dr. Guevera promptly put his Beethoven hairs in a sterile petri dish and locked it in his office safe. He then found two scientists to perform the tests: Dr. Werner Baumgartner, head of the Psychemedics Corporation in Culver City, California, near Los Angeles; and William Walsh, director of the Health Research Institute in Naperville, Illinois.

Baumgartner had tested more than 2 million hairs since 1977, employing a patented process of radioimmunoassay now commonly used by police departments nationwide. In 1986 Baumgartner had found high

Illustration 3.4   **Beethoven's Hair**

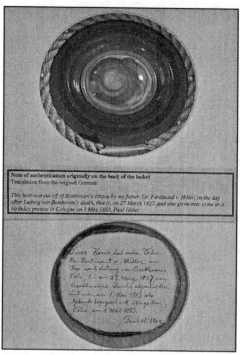

Two U.S. collectors, Ira Brilliant and Alfredo
Guevara, shared a lock of Beethoven's hair, this
one from Brilliant's Center for Beethoven Studies
in San Jose, California. Did the great composer die
of lead poisoning?

morphine levels in the hair of English poet John Keats, consistent with
the poet's known use of drugs. Normally Baumgartner would wash hair
specimens in dry ethanol at a temperature of 37 degrees. After additional
washing and drying, they would be tested for chemical contents. In the
case of Beethoven's hair, Baumgartner in May 1996 found no morphine
or other opium derivative in his sample, suggesting that Beethoven must
have used something else to cope with the pain that racked his body
during his final years.

William Walsh was a chemical engineer with a PhD from Iowa State
University who had become an expert on hair analysis and autism. In
the early 1970s, he worked at the Institute for Atomic Research at Ames,

Iowa, and then at Los Alamos National Laboratory in New Mexico. He then worked at the Argonne National Laboratory outside Chicago, where he helped process nuclear fuels and tested prison inmates for trace metals in their hair. In 1976 Walsh left Argonne and established his own company, Health Research Institute.

In May 1996 Walsh received twenty sample Beethoven hairs for his laboratory. He promptly subcontracted the testing to the nationally known microscopist Walter McCrone, now eighty-three, whose McCrone Research Institute in Chicago had previously tested Napoleon's hair, the Vinland Map, and the Shroud of Turin. McCrone incinerated the hairs in a low-temperature nascent oxygen asher, then analyzed the ash from five hairs using scanning electron microscope energy dispersion spectrometry, mercifully abbreviated to SEM/EDS. He quickly found that Beethoven's hairs had an unusually high level of lead. But the results were not definitive or conclusive enough to publish.

In the summer of 1999, scientists at LabCorp in North Carolina also determined the genetic composition of Beethoven's hair using mitochondrial DNA sequencing.

The case of Beethoven's hair rested there until 2000, when writer Russell Martin produced a full-length study titled *Beethoven's Hair* that tracked the famous lock from the composer's head through Germany and Denmark to its current homes in Arizona and California. Spurred by public interest, a team of Argonne Laboratory scientists decided to replicate the McCrone-Walsh study. Argonne had a new synchrotron, a set of powerful magnets that used radio-frequency waves to accelerate electrons around a ring at nearly the speed of light. The scientists decided to utilize the synchrotron to study Beethoven's hair.

In the fall of 2000, Kenneth Kemner, an Argonne scientist working with his colleagues Derrick Mancini and Francesco DeCarlo, discovered high lead levels that confirmed the earlier McCrone-Walsh results. They discovered in a few hours that lead levels were unusually high (60 ppm) both on the outside and inside of the six hairs they were testing. It was a "Eureka!" moment. "I'm driving home at one in the morning by myself," Kemner recalled, "thinking 'There's four people in the world who know why Beethoven died.' And I did it." Kemner went home, put on a recording of Beethoven's Ninth Symphony, and cried. But he was sworn to secrecy about what he had discovered.

Two years later Argonne scientists again confirmed the earlier high lead levels using an advanced photon source (APS) machine. They also used x-ray fluorescence from an SRI-CAT beam-line. Beethoven's lead levels were 100 times the normal. He had evidently died of lead poisoning. But what was the source of the lead?

In May 2005, filmmakers showed up at Argonne to shoot scenes for the forthcoming film *Beethoven's Hair* that reenacted the 2000 experiment by Kemner. In a December interview with Jeffrey Brown on the PBS *NewsHour*, Walsh confirmed that Beethoven exhibited traits of lead poisoning since he was in his twenties. Again, the prime researcher was Ken Kemner, who had run six more hours of tests on hair samples.

In addition, the scientists found elevated lead in bone fragments from Beethoven (exhumed in 1863) owned by Paul Kaufman, a California businessman, who had inherited them from his great-uncle, an Austrian doctor. Two Vienna physicians had studied the fragments in the 1980s. Scientists at the Institute of Legal Medicine at the University of Muenster, Germany, in the summer of 2005 compared the mitochondrial DNA in the bone fragments with that from Beethoven's hair studied in North Carolina in 1999 and got a perfect match. The hair definitely belonged to Beethoven.

"The fact that we saw the lead in the bone and hair tells us, this was a chronic exposure," Kemner recalled in 2007. "It's clear this wasn't a large amount of lead that hit poor Beethoven at once and then he died. It had already settled into his bones and the way the body gets rid of heavy metals like lead is through the hair and fingernails."

Beethoven had long suffered from bad digestion, chronic stomach pains, irritability, and depression. Scientists knew that chronic lead poisoning results in abdominal pain, muscle weakness, fatigue, and irritability. And we know Beethoven came in contact with lead in his favorite ceramic goblet, in sugar used as a wine sweetener, in house paint, and in his many pencils used in composition. Perhaps these many sources added up to high levels of lead.

But hold on! In 2010 Dr. Albert C. Todd, an expert on lead poisoning at Mount Sinai School of Medicine in New York, ran tests on pieces of Beethoven's skull (again from Brilliant and Guevara's collection) and found no more lead than normally expected. Todd concluded that "Beethoven didn't have long-term high lead exposure." Walsh responded that Todd's tests involved measurements with x-ray fluorescence, measurements that were not nearly as accurate as the Argonne tests.

What's a layman to believe when the experts disagree? Perhaps only that the case is still open. Beethoven was wracked by pain during his last years, and we simply don't know exactly how lead poisoning may have played into the drama. Beethoven had clearly died in great suffering in 1827. But the reasons remain as debatable among historians and musicologists as among the scientists. The beat goes on.

Napoleon's hair had been tested for arsenic at Harwell during the early days of neutron activation analysis. By the time Vincent Guinn tested the Kennedy bullets (1977) and Oak Ridge scientists looked for arsenic in Zachary Taylor's bones and hair (1991), the technique was well known. Beethoven's hair underwent even more sophisticated testing with advanced technology at Argonne. Yet for every scientific opinion on the matter, there appeared to be an opposing view. Forensic science was almost as much of an argument without end as forensic history—and history.

In 2012 there was a coda to the composition regarding Beethoven's hair and the story of how atomic evidence was used to study lead levels. A composer in Scotland, Stuart Mitchell, was an expert on "cymatics," the study of sound and vibration. He assigned one musical note to each of the twenty-two amino acids found in Beethoven's DNA sequence. He then composed a piece for viola and piano using only those twenty-two notes and called it "Ludwig's Last Song." Maybe it was Beethoven's last, or maybe not. Time will tell.

References

3.1 For a general analysis of Napoleon's hair and other mysteries, see Peter Haugen, *Was Napoleon Poisoned? And Other Unsolved Mysteries of Royal History* (Hoboken, NJ: John Wiley, 2008). On Sten Forshufvud and Napoleon's hair, see Sten Forshufvud and Ben Weider, *Assassination at St. Helena Revisited* (New York: John Wiley, 1995), especially pp. 480–494. Later analyses of the debate include the article "Napoleon's Death by Arsenic Exposure?" at www.toxipedia.org/pages/viewpage.action/pageId.7962 and William J. Broad, "Hair Analyses Deflates Napoleon Poisoning Theories," *New York Times*, June 10, 2008.

3.2 There are hundreds of books on the Kennedy assassination. A solid and sensible survey of many of them is by Michael L. Kurtz, *The JFK Assassination Debates: Lone Gunman versus Conspiracy* (Lawrence: University Press of Kansas, 2006). The best source on Vincent Guinn and his testimony before the HSCA is Kenneth B. Rahn, *The Academic JFK Assassination Site*, www.Kenrahn.com/JFK/JFK.html. A good biography of Guinn is by his colleagues George E. Miller, David A. Miller, and F. Sherwood Rowland, "In Memoriam: Vincent Perrie Guinn," www.universityofcalifornia. edu/senate/inmemoriam.

The ballistic case for a second shooter is G. Paul Chambers, *Head Shot: The Science behind the JFK Assassination* (New York: Prometheus Books, 2010). On the cinematic evidence, see David R. Wrone, *The Zapruder Film: Reframing JFK's Assassination* (Lawrence: University Press of Kansas, 2003). Gerald Posner's *Case Closed: Lee Harvey Oswald and the Assassination of John F. Kennedy* (New York: Random House, 1993) is the best attempt to close a case that will probably forever remain open.

3.3 The best account of the Zachary Taylor exhumation and testing is in William R. Maples, *Dead Men Do Tell Tales* (New York: Doubleday, 1994), 223–237. See also the *New York Times* coverage of the exhumation (June 27, 1991). A revisionist critique of the whole affair appears in *History as Mystery* by Michael Parenti (San Francisco: City Lights Books, 1999), 209–239.

3.4 On William Walsh and Beethoven's hair, see Russell Martin, *Beethoven's Hair* (New York: Broadway Books, 2000). For an account of the more recent forensic analysis, read Russell Martin and Linda Nibley, *The Mysteries of Beethoven's Hair* (Watertown, MA: Charlesbridge, 2009). I have also drawn on the interview with Ken Kemner, "The Day the Music Died," in *Saskatoon StarPhoenix*, June 18, 2007, and on James Barron, "Beethoven May Not Have Died of Lead Poisoning After All," *New York Times*, May 28, 2010.

A Question of Identity

From Bones to DNA Fingerprinting

Forensic scientists often have to decide questions of identity, that is, whether a person really is who that person is alleged to be. Forensic scientists study dead individuals who cannot tell us who they are except through their bones or DNA. In the 1980s Dr. Mildred Trotter's techniques and formulas of using the lengths of long bones to confirm or calculate height, gender, race, and weight still remained useful. But in the mid-1980s, forensic scientists discovered an entirely novel technique for taking samples of DNA from bones, blood, or hair to identify an individual. The British discoverer of the technique, Alec Jeffreys, called it DNA fingerprinting.

Jeffreys had his "Eureka moment" in his University of Leicester laboratory at 10 a.m. on Monday, September 10, 1984, when he saw x-ray film that clearly showed both similarities and differences between the DNA of two different members of the same family. He quickly realized he had a new tool to prove or disprove identity.

The U.S. House Select Committee on Assassinations had assembled forensics experts in the 1970s to review evidence on the murders of John Kennedy, Robert Kennedy, and Martin Luther King Jr. In the 1980s, forensic veterans like Clyde Snow, Ellis Kerley, Vincent Guinn, William Maples, Michael Baden, and Lowell Levine worked on other cases involving well-known historical figures and identifying airline crash passengers and the bones of family members who "disappeared" in civil wars in the former Yugoslavia and Latin America. These scientists were all members of the forensic anthropology section of the American Academy of Forensic Sciences, established in 1973. Some called themselves the "Last Word Society" and delighted in investigating historical mysteries of the famous dead and reporting their findings with good humor at annual gatherings. They were inventing forensic history.

Forensics was all the rage after 1976 when the TV series *Quincy, M.E.*, starring Jack Klugman, portrayed a Los Angeles medical examiner and forensic pathologist as a crime-buster. Quincy employed science to outwit the police in solving murder cases. Another program titled *The New Detectives: Case Studies in Forensic Science* ran on the Discovery Channel about twenty years later. Both programs anticipated the even more popular *CSI (Crime Scene Investigation)* series that began in 2000 and portrayed forensics at work in New York, Los Angeles, Miami, and Las Vegas. *CSI* still commands a broad audience. So does *Cold Case*.

The major shift in forensic techniques from bone pathology to DNA fingerprinting first became apparent with the discovery and identification of Josef Mengele, the Nazi doctor known as the "Angel of Death" thanks to his medical experiments on living individuals at Auschwitz concentration camp during World War II. Forensic pathology strongly suggested that the bones found in Brazil were Mengele's, but only DNA tests later confirmed that they were indeed his. Then came the exhumed bones of the Romanov family, murdered in 1918, analyzed first by odontology and bone forensics, and then subsequently confirmed by DNA fingerprinting that identified the entire family, including Nicholas and Alexandra's youngest daughter, Anastasia. Thomas Jefferson's relationship with his slave, Sally Hemings, also became the sensational topic of a debate over the results of DNA testing, proving only that a Jefferson male, not necessarily Thomas, had fathered children by Sally.

The last king of France, Louis XVII, who died in prison at the age of ten, also was finally put to rest by DNA confirmation of his identity and the identities of various false pretenders. Hitler's skull, exhibited in Moscow in 2000, presented another forensic challenge of identification. Geneticist Linda Strausbaugh at the University of Connecticut solved the problem only in 2009 when she discovered that the DNA of "Hitler's skull" belonged to a woman under forty.

By the twenty-first century, DNA fingerprinting had become a major tool in the toolbox of forensics and even of history. And in each case of forensic history, the media tended to jump to conclusions before the scientists had completed their tests. Forensic scientists wanted empirical conclusions based on evidence. Journalists wanted a big story based on the latest sound bite.

4.1 Clyde Snow: Identifying the "Angel of Death"

"Bones make good witnesses," Clyde Snow once wrote. "They may speak softly, but they don't lie and they never forget."

In 1979 Josef Mengele, the Nazi "Angel of Death," who experimented on human beings—notably twins—at Auschwitz during World War II, drowned while hiding out in Brazil under an alias. Only in 1985 did the woman who buried Mengele disclose his true identity to authorities. Leading American forensic anthropologist Clyde Snow had identified the remains of Chicago serial killer John Wayne Gacy's victims, the U.S. soldiers killed at Custer's Last Stand, air crash passenger victims, and the "disappeared" in Argentina's civil war. In June 1985, Snow led one of four international teams (two from the United States, one from Germany and one from Israel) that finally proved that the dead Mengele was in fact the Nazi Josef Mengele by using old photographs, skull and facial reconstruction, and dental x-rays. But only a DNA match with Mengele's surviving brother in Germany closed the case.

Clyde Snow's work in Argentina and Brazil led him to help in the identification of the alleged remains of Butch Cassidy and the Sundance Kid—outlaw heroes memorialized in a Paul Newman and Robert Redford movie—in Bolivia. The two fugitives supposedly perished at the hands of the Bolivian army about 1910, but their remains were never found. In December 1991, Snow helped examine exhumed bones and skulls. A DNA sample from Sundance's brother in Pennsylvania, exhumed for the purpose, determined that the Brazilian bones were those of a German miner, not the two outlaws, just as the miner's tombstone alleged. No one really knew where Butch and the Kid had been buried or how they died.

Born in 1928, Clyde Snow grew up in the Texas Panhandle in the 1930s, son of a country doctor who took young Clyde with him on visits to crime scenes and autopsies. After receiving his BS degree from Eastern New Mexico State in anthropology in 1951, Snow attended Baylor University medical school for two years and then received an MS in zoology from Texas Tech in 1955. After three years in the air force, he undertook graduate study in archaeology at the University of Arizona. He then worked in the 1960s for the Federal Aviation Administration (FAA) identifying passenger remains following airplane crashes. Married and divorced three times, Snow learned forensic science as he went along, training himself to become what he called one of the "archivists of death." He trained in the era of bone pathology, but would continue working into the age of DNA.

On May 25, 1979, American Airlines Flight 191 crashed after taking off from O'Hare Airport in Chicago, killing 258 passengers, 13 crew members, and two people on the ground—the deadliest air crash in U.S. history. The FAA promptly brought in Clyde Snow and odontologist Lowell Levine—a voluble, bearded consultant to the New York City medical examiner's office. Within five weeks, their team had identified all but 29 bodies of the 273 people killed in the crash. Snow had just finished identifying the victims of serial killer John Wayne Gacy when the crash occurred, and it is understandable that he decided to take early retirement from his FAA work in 1980 at the age of fifty-two.

Since 1976 Snow had worked on identifying the "disappeared" (*desaparacidas*) in the civil war in Argentina. In 1984 he formed the Argentina Forensic Anthropology Team (EAAF) to work on victims of human rights abuses. Within a short time the team expanded its work to include the killing fields and graveyards of Bosnia, East Timor, El Salvador, Guatemala, and Zimbabwe. As part of this effort, Snow returned to Argentina in February 1985 to direct a five-week training workshop on how to identify skeletal remains. Lowell Levine again joined Snow as the resident odontologist.

In May, Clyde Snow was at the battlefield of the Little Bighorn River in southern Montana identifying the bones of some of Custer's soldiers that were discovered in August 1983 after a prairie fire swept through the area. Here he utilized Mildred Trotter's method of calculating the height of people by measuring their long bones. Then in June 1985, Snow got a call from Brazil asking if he could join two other forensic scientists—Lowell Levine and Ellis Kerley—in authenticating the newly discovered bones allegedly belonging to Josef Mengele, the notorious Nazi "Angel of Death."

Ellis R. Kerley (1924–1998) was a Canadian-born pioneer in forensic anthropology. After army service during World War II, Kerley helped identify the remains of soldiers from the wars in Korea and Vietnam at the Armed Forces Institute of Pathology. He also served with Snow, Levine, and others on the House Select Committee on Assassinations forensic team. In addition, Kerley investigated bodies found at Jonestown in Guyana after a mass religious suicide and the victims of the failed Iran hostage raid by American soldiers in 1980. By 1985 Kerley was employed by the U.S. Marshals Service.

In June 1985, Romeu Toma, federal police chief of São Paulo, Brazil, watched as gravediggers unearthed a moldy coffin from the ground near the village of Embu. Two German émigrés, Wolfram and Liselotte Bossert, observed the exhumation. Liselotte had recently told the Brazilian police that in 1979 she had helped bury a man known as "Wolfgang Gerhard," although she knew that his real name was Josef Mengele, the notorious Nazi commandant from Auschwitz. Now she watched as Dr. José Antonio de Mello, assistant director of the local police forensic lab, placed the bones in a large plastic box, held up a skull for the television cameras, and headlined the world news that night.

But was the body really that of Mengele? The police knew that Mengele had fled Germany to Argentina in 1949 and had eluded capture after the trial of Adolf Eichmann, another Nazi war criminal, in 1961. As the "Angel of Death," Mengele had helped kill 400,000 men, women, and children at Auschwitz and conducted medical experiments on human subjects. These involved electroshocks, radiation exposure, and bone marrow transplants. Captured and then freed by the U.S. Army in 1945, Mengele hid out at a farm in Bavaria for several years before escaping to South America. There were frequent "Mengele sightings" worldwide for years as Israeli intelligence tried to hunt the Nazi murderer down. The Bosserts had befriended him in exile and kept his identity secret, even when "Wolfgang Gerhard," as Mengele was known, drowned swimming in the ocean off Brazil in 1979. After the Bosserts finally led police to Mengele's grave in Embu, de Mello and teams sent by the United States, Germany, and Israel began to investigate whether or not Josef Mengele was really the body in custody.

The scientific teams were impressive. Israeli intelligence worked with the U.S. Marshals Service hunting Mengele and found that the federal marshals claimed the right to search for evidence on foreign soil. The U.S. Department of Justice asked Ellis Kerley and Lowell Levine to represent the United States in the case. (Kerley had previously misidentified another man as Mengele in a photograph.) The West German team included Rolf Endris, an odontologist from Mainz, and Richard Helmer, an expert on skull-face superposition from Kiel who had worked with Clyde Snow on passenger identification in the past. The Mengele case gained worldwide attention, and the fiasco of the "Hitler Diaries" two years earlier cautioned scientists against reaching premature conclusions under pressure from journalists and the media.

Illustration 4.1   **Josef Mengele**

The Nazi murderer Josef Mengele in Buenos Aires
in 1956. Were the bones really his?

On June 14, 1985, Clyde Snow flew from Oklahoma City to Brazil
and arrived in São Paulo only to confront a mob of reporters and TV
cameras. "Welcome to the Barnum & Bailey Sideshow," joked Snow.
He soon met up with Kerley and Levine, who had procured Mengele's
SS records, including his 1938 physical examination report, from the
Berlin Documentation Center. One key finding was that Mengele had
a bone disease known as septia osteomyelitis as a teenager and had
an operation performed on his right leg bone. Kerley had found this
condition among some of the three thousand bone-sets of soldiers he
examined at the Armed Forces Institute of Pathology and understood
the disease.

The foreign scientists began to examine the exhumed bones and
skull under Brazilian supervision. Forensic analysis confirmed that the
body was that of a male (narrow and steep pelvis) in his late sixties

(femur blood-carrying canals [osteons] and tooth abrasions) who was Caucasian (eye sockets and nose) and right-handed (bones longer on the right than on the left side). According to Mengele's old SS file, he was a white male 174 centimeters (5' 8") tall with a head circumference of 57 centimeters (22.4"). His 1938 dental chart showed twelve fillings, but without location. Using Mildred Trotter's formula for determining height and measuring the length of the femur, tibia, and humerus bones, the scientists calculated that the buried man had a height of 173.5 centimeters. Teeth x-rays examined by Levine showed a wide incisor canal on the upper palate typical of gap teeth—which Mengele possessed and which were apparent in his earlier photographs. The Bosserts had described Mengele as about age sixty-eight when he drowned in 1979, and the SS records confirmed that Mengele was born in 1911.

Richard Helmer applied skull-face superposition techniques that Clyde Snow had used to identify some of Custer's soldiers a few months earlier. The techniques had been first used in the 1930s, but were only widespread after 1976. The question was: did the skull found at Embu match the SS photos of Mengele in 1938 when the Nazi was twenty-seven years old? The trick was to find thirty points on the skull, mount pins secured with clay, and mount the skull on an adjustable tripod. Rubber sheeting over the pins approximated the face on the skull, following Gerasimov's facial reconstruction techniques of an earlier day. A video camera on tracks sent images to an image processor and then a television monitor. Here the skull points were superimposed over photographs of Mengele. The result was a perfect match. "Now you see," said a jubilant Helmer, "that this isn't fantasy . . . this is Josef Mengele." Levine's comparison of the teeth with 1978 dental records of the deceased "Wolfgang Gerhard" offered further confirmation. Levine concluded "with an absolute certainty" that this was Mengele.

But there was as yet no evidence of the osteomyelitis that Mengele was known to have suffered from as a boy. The lack of evidence recommended caution. When Snow and Kerley drafted the report concluding that "this skeleton is that of Josef Mengele," they added the phrase "within a reasonable scientific certainty." The press jumped to the conclusion that Mengele had been found, but the Israelis sent physical anthropologist Donald Ortner of the Smithsonian Institution to Brazil in January 1986 to confirm the results. Still there was no evidence of the osteomyelitis. Finally, in 1989, West German prosecutor Hans Klein turned to British geneticists Alec Jeffreys and Erika Hagelberg for a DNA fingerprinting test on the Mengele remains.

The test was quite new. In April 1990, Erika Hagelberg extracted trace amounts of DNA from the femur and humerus bones found in the body unearthed at Embu. Jeffreys put them in storage. The West Germans were finally able to get blood samples from Mengele's widow Irene Hackenjos and from his son Rolf, who had previously refused to cooperate. On February 12, 1992, the samples were given to Jeffreys at his laboratory at the University of Leicester. Jeffreys removed the Embu DNA samples from storage, compared them with the blood samples, and concluded that Mengele and Rolf were "beyond reasonable doubt" father and son. In the autumn of 1992, U.S., West German, and Israeli authorities finally closed the case on Josef Mengele using DNA.

Mengele's case in 1985 brought together forensic scientists who employed their usual pathology tests on bones, teeth, and skull to establish identity. But the final proof was established only seven years later with the aid of DNA. The same shift from traditional pathology to DNA fingerprinting would prove to be crucial in identifying the bones of the last Romanov rulers of Russia. Forensics was moving from pathology to DNA fingerprinting, and the standard of proof was changing in laboratories and courtrooms around the world. Forensic history was evolving.

4.2 Peter Gill: Romanov Bones and DNA Matches

Forensic history can be a bloody business. Another identity case involving the use of DNA analysis after the collapse of the Soviet Union in 1991 confirmed that all the Romanov family members present died in the mass shooting of July 1918, that Nicholas and Alexandra's youngest children Anastasia and Aleksei were among them, and that pretender Anna Anderson's DNA did not match that of the Romanovs and their nearest living blood relative, Prince Philip, Duke of Edinburgh. Lenin ordered all the Romanovs in Ekaterinburg murdered, and they were. Peter Gill of the British Forensic Science Service (BFSS) identified the bodies definitively with DNA analysis beginning in 1994 and ending in 2008. Any "Anastasia" was a pretender.

Historical conventional wisdom held that the family of Tsar Nicholas II and some of their retainers had been machine-gunned for twenty-one minutes in the basement of a Siberian mansion in Ekaterinburg, known as the House of Special Designation, in the early morning hours of July 17, 1918, as White troops approached the city. A Fiat truck engine roared to muffle the sound of the fusillade. On the night of July 17–18, according to a story told to journalist Richard Halliburton by one of the killers in 1935, the bodies were reportedly doused in acid and gasoline, burned, and buried in a nearby mineshaft. The only problem was that during the entire period that the Soviet Union existed, nobody had produced the bones of the last Romanovs. Where were they? And had anyone possibly escaped the carnage?

In 1979 Alexander Avdonin, a geologist, and Geli Ryabov, a film-maker, and their wives discovered some of the Romanov remains at Koptyaki, a village some twelve miles northwest of Ekaterinburg. The site had been identified earlier in a secret report of Yakov Yurovsky, the Bolshevik in charge of killing the Imperial family. Avdonin and Ryabov kept their discovery a secret for a decade until Ryabov, in an interview on April 10, 1989, announced that he had discovered the burial site of the Romanovs. With the collapse of the Soviet Union, Russian president Boris Yeltsin promptly announced that the government would direct the exhumation and scientific analysis of the bones of the royal family.

On July 11, 1991, Avdonin and a team arrived in military trucks and, after three days of digging, found nine skeletons, apparently four males and five females. The remains were laid out on the floor of a police firing range in Ekaterinburg. Sergei Abramov, the leading forensic scientist at the Russian Ministry of Health in Moscow, took over the task of analyzing some 500 bones, skulls, and pieces of bones. (A second exhumation in October 1991 turned up 300 bone fragments and 150 pieces of tissue, rope, and ceramic pieces.) The Russians knew little about DNA analysis and, at any rate, there was no money available to fund genetic tests. Using Gerasimov's techniques and a video camera, the Russians matched skull formations with old photographs and used a computer to calculate the probability of a match. They also used Mildred Trotter's formulas for long bones to calculate the gender, age, race, and height of each skeleton.

William Maples later criticized the Russian exhumation as "badly conceived" and conducted in a "poor manner." Nonetheless, the Russian team identified nine bodies as follows: (1) Anna S. Demidova, maid; (2) Dr. Evgeny S. Botkin, physician; (3) Grand Duchess Olga; (4) Emperor Nicholas II; (5) Grand Duchess Marie; (6) Grand Duchess Tatiana; (7) Empress Alexandra; (8) Ivan M. Kharitonov, cook; (9) Aleksei I. Trupp,

Illustration 4.2a   **the Romanov Family, 1913**

DNA fingerprinting proved that Nicholas II and his family were all machine-gunned to death in 1918 and that the "Anastasia" living in Virginia was an impostor.

valet. The bodies of the Tsarevich Aleksei and Grand Duchess Anastasia appeared to be missing.

The Russians had made little additional progress by February 1992 when U.S. Secretary of State James Baker arrived in Ekaterinburg on a state visit, viewed the bones, and offered to send an American team of forensics experts to assist the Russians, the team to be headed by government scientist Richard Froede. But the Russians wanted a different team headed by William Maples, the forensic anthropologist who ran the C.A. Pound Human Identification Laboratory at the University of Florida in Gainesville. The Russians knew that Maples was well qualified: he identified the remains of Spanish explorer Francisco Pizarro in 1984 and in 1991 had helped exhume the remains of U.S. president Zachary Taylor.

Maples's team comprised well-known experts—Michael Baden, Lowell Levine, Catherine Oakes—Levine's wife and a hair-and-fiber microscopist with the New York State Police—and several more colleagues of Maples from the University of Florida. Levine was president of the American Academy of Forensic Odontology, taught at the School of Dentistry at New York University, and had helped identify MIAs in Vietnam and the serial killer Ted Bundy, as well as Josef Mengele. Maples, Levine, and Baden had all worked together with Ellis Kerley at the U.S. Army's Central Identification Laboratory in Hawaii (where Mildred Trotter had done her pioneering work). Since 1986, Baden, Levine, Kerley, and Maples constituted the New York state police Forensic Science Unit. The U.S. State Department ultimately allowed the unit (paying its own expenses) to head up the Romanov remains investigation.

When Maples and his team arrived in Ekaterinburg in July 1992, they were taken by surprise. The Russians "had no modern techniques or methodology." They were using facial recognition techniques developed in the 1930s by Gerasimov and Bernard Spillsbury in England. Nevertheless, Baden and Levine promptly agreed with the Russians, based on the bones and dental evidence from molars and wisdom teeth, that the missing bodies were those of Aleksei and Anastasia. "We knew that we were dealing with the remains of the Imperial family," wrote Maples later, "and we knew which one was which."

Levine's dental examination was especially important. He identified Alexandra by the excellent teeth she had thanks to dental care in Germany before World War I. He was able to confirm the Russian identification of all nine bodies by further dental investigation. Throughout the procedure Levine remained the quiet, cool, and unruffled professional with whom Baden had worked for thirty years.

In 1992 Eduard Radzinsky published his book *The Last Tsar*, using the "Yurovsky Note" by the lead executioner, a note that Yurovsky's son had kept hidden for all these years. Yurovsky described the carnage caused by twelve men firing Mauser, Nagant, and Browning machine pistols at close range, and the burial of the bodies in a pit dug in a bog, the same pit discovered by Avdonin and Ryabov in 1979. The killers had first tried to cremate the bodies with gasoline, but the temperature of the fire was too low. They then moved the remains to a mineshaft known locally as the Four Brothers, threw acid on them, and finally moved them again to the bog site near a railroad line.

But the case remained open pending DNA analysis and the discovery of the other two bodies a number of years later. In the autumn of 1992, the Russian government signed an agreement with the British Home Office Laboratories and Forensic Science Services to test the Romanov remains using their DNA. Pavel Ivanov of the Engelhardt Institute of Molecular Biology in Moscow flew to London in September with sections of femurs and tibias of all nine skeletons. Ivanov had already visited the Central Criminal Research Center at Aldermaston in December 1991 to negotiate the DNA testing. His coworkers would be Peter Gill, director of the Molecular Research Center of the Forensic Science Services (FSS), and Alec Jeffreys, the inventor of DNA fingerprinting. Ivanov drove to Gill's home near Aldermaston with all the Romanov bone and teeth samples in his travel bag. (Aldermaston was primarily a nuclear research facility operated by the Ministry of Defense.)

Peter Gill was then in his early forties, of slight build, with a moustache and glasses. After studying zoology at Bristol University, Gill went on to get his PhD in genetics at Liverpool University. After a five-year postdoctoral position at Nottingham, he began working for FSS in 1982. A few years later he joined Alec Jeffreys's laboratory at the University of Leicester and began to work on DNA fingerprinting. Ivanov had asked Gill to test the Romanov bones using probes—radioactive isotopes that produce a film image of DNA strands.

DNA typing, or fingerprinting, is based on the sequence of bases that make up DNA. A long strand is better than a short one for purposes of analysis. Each person's DNA—but only about 2 percent—is unique to that individual. The remainder is common to the human genome. There are two types of sequence: (1) variable number tandem repeats (VNTR), and (2) short tandem repeats (STR) that contain three to seven base pairs. Identification means finding the same repeat patterns at multiple places in the DNA that defines an individual.

To analyze the DNA, a technician needs to separate it and cut it into segments, again separating fragments using electrophoresis, transferring them to a nylon membrane that shows bands similar to a bar code. The bands are made visible by radioisotopes in an autoradiograph that clearly shows if the bar codes from two samples do or do not match.

Over a ten-month period, the Gill-Ivanov team used polymerase chain reaction (PCR) techniques to confirm that the bones were those of four males and five females and that five were from the same family. Short tandem repeats of base pairs showed that bodies 4 and 7 were the parents of bodies 3, 5, and 6. The scientists guessed that Tsarevich Aleksei and one of the daughters were missing, probably the youngest, Anastasia.

Illustration 4.2b   **Alec Jeffreys**

Alec Jeffreys, the pioneer in DNA fingerprinting at the University of Leicester, England, oversaw Peter Gill's DNA typing of the Romanov remains in the 1990s.

Gill's team then sequenced the base pairs of DNA and compared the DNA from Alexandra and three of her daughters with the DNA of Prince Philip, Duke of Edinburgh, grandnephew of Tsarina Alexandra. Philip donated a blood sample of five cubic centimeters whose mtDNA (mitochondrial DNA, found only in the maternal line) was a perfect match.

Philip's DNA was important. Both he and his wife Queen Elizabeth were great-great-grandchildren of Queen Victoria. Philip's maternal grandmother, Victoria, was Tsarina Alexandra's sister. Through his mother and grandmother, Philip carried the same mitochondrial DNA as the Romanovs.

The mtDNA is found not in the cell nucleus, but in the surrounding mitochondria, the small organelles in the cytoplasm that produce energy. That mtDNA passes from one generation to another only through the mothers, is located where no nuclear DNA exists, is very hardy, and is inherited unchanged over time.

In July 1993, Gill and Ivanov announced their results. They were 98.5 percent certain that the bones were from the Romanov family. Maples, who met Gill for the first time at the press conference, was annoyed at Gill's premature announcement, which Maples considered a "glory grab." The test results, thought Maples, should have been first sent to Moscow for confirmation and announcement. On the other hand, Ivanov was indignant that Maples and Levine had taken bone and teeth samples to the California laboratory of geneticist Mary-Claire King for DNA study. Maples in November signed an affidavit stating that the identification of the Romanov remains could not be judged definitive. The scientists were at odds.

But there was more evidence. Nicholas's younger brother George had died of tuberculosis in 1899 at the age of twenty-eight and was buried in the Peter and Paul Fortress in St. Petersburg. In May 1995, the Russian government sent Ivanov with bone and blood samples of George to the Armed Forces Institute of Pathology in Rockville, Maryland, for analysis. The samples were gene sequenced and their mtDNA compared with body 4 (Nicholas II) at Gill's laboratory. They matched exactly, both having a rare condition known as heteroplasmy, where two types of mtDNA appear in the same person.

Ivanov also brought along to Rockville samples of the blood-soaked shirt and handkerchief of Nicholas II retrieved from a botched assassination attempt on the future emperor's life in Japan in 1892. Ivanov had traveled to Japan and recovered samples, but in this case they were too contaminated to analyze.

DNA evidence also showed that Anna Anderson (1896–1984), the woman who claimed for years to be Anastasia, was only a pretender to the throne in the best Russian tradition. Russian history was littered with tales of false Dmitrys, Peters, and Alexanders. They usually turned up after the death of a tsar and claimed to have survived some violent event. Anna Anderson was in fact a Polish peasant named Francisca Schanzkowska, fished out of the Landwehr Canal in Berlin in 1920 after a failed suicide attempt. But she thought she was Anastasia.

After emigrating to the United States, Anderson had married a college history professor named Jack Manahan (in order to get a U.S. visa). The two lived together in Charlottesville, Virginia, with a houseful of cats and dogs for many years as reclusive eccentrics. In 1979 Anna Manahan had an operation at a Charlottesville hospital, which kept her tissue samples. These, along with some of her hairs kept by Jack Manahan in an envelope, preserved her mtDNA. When tested in 1994, the samples proved conclusively that Anna Manahan was not a Romanov but was, in fact, related to Karl Maucher, a living grand-nephew of the Polish woman Francisca Schanzkowska. Over the years she had apparently convinced herself that she really was Anastasia, but she was not. Case closed.

In 1998, on the eightieth anniversary of the murders, the Romanov remains were buried together in the St. Catherine's chapel of the Peter and Paul Fortress. Two years later the Romanov's were canonized as saints of the Russian Orthodox Church and martyrs for the faith, or "passion bearers."

But doubts remained. In August 2001, Japanese scientists examined the DNA blood samples of Tikhon Kulikovsky, a nephew of Nicholas II who had died in Toronto. The Japanese concluded that the DNA was not that of the Romanov family. In 2004 Alec Knight and Joanna Mountain at Stanford University claimed that a long sequence of 1,223 bases could not be obtained from seventy-year-old bones. They analyzed a finger of the Grand Duchess Elizabeth (Alexandra's older sister, executed in 1918) and concluded that the bones examined by Gill and Ivanov might well not be the Romanov remains. Peter Gill called the conclusion vindictive and political.

There was more digging and searching at Ganina Yama, the pit where the bodies had been found, without any new discoveries. Then in July 2007, two more bodies were found in Pig's Meadow at the Porosenkov Ravine, four and a half miles away from the pit. Only in March 2009 did Dr. Michael Coble and other scientists at the U.S. Armed Forces DNA Identification Laboratory confirm on the basis of DNA analysis that these were the remains of Aleksei and Anastasia.

The case of the Romanovs shows how forensic and historical evidence are intertwined. The initial task was to find the family's remains, an arduous search lasting from 1979 to 2008. Identification of the eleven bodies at first involved the well-known techniques of forensic pathology, notably facial recognition and the measurement of bones, teeth, and skulls. In the end, DNA typing produced new historical conclusions: all the members of the Romanov entourage had been murdered in July 1918, and the various "Anastasias" that had surfaced over the years, including Anna Anderson, were simply pretenders who believed, or fulfilled, a romantic dream that at least one Romanov had escaped the bloody carnage in the basement of the house in Ekaterinburg. None had, as we now know.

Thanks to forensics, DNA fingerprinting, and forensic history, we can now say conclusively that Nicholas II and his family were indeed all murdered on that dreadful night in 1918. Bones don't lie. Neither does DNA. Case closed.

4.3 Eugene Foster: Jefferson's Children

Charlottesville, Virginia, featured another DNA announcement in 1998. Not only was Anna Manahan not Anastasia, but Thomas Jefferson might well have fathered a child by one of his slaves.

Ever since U.S. president Thomas Jefferson's lifetime, people had argued whether he had fathered children by one of his slaves, Sally Hemings. Retired pathologist Eugene Foster's 1998 DNA tests of Jefferson's and Hemings's male descendants and relatives seemed to show the presence of the same Y-chromosome DNA alleles. A few historians like Joseph Ellis changed their minds on the paternity issue because of modern science. They thought Thomas Jefferson might well have fathered children by Hemings. Most scientists concluded only that one or more Jefferson males (of two dozen in Virginia)—including Thomas, his brothers, and his cousins—fathered Sally's children. Foster's DNA tests were misunderstood, and the paternity case against Jefferson remains unproven.

As early as 1802, a muckraking journalist named James Callender charged that Jefferson and Sally Hemings had a seven-year-old son, Tom, who was conceived in Paris in 1795 when Jefferson was serving as U.S. minister there. Callender was a self-confessed liar, a racist, a drunkard, and a defamer of five presidents. But his allegations against Jefferson and "dusky Sally" persisted.

In 1998 a retired pathologist in Charlottesville named Eugene Foster (1927–2008) learned of the recent progress in DNA fingerprinting to prove identity. Foster was born in the Bronx, got his medical degree from Washington University in St. Louis (where Mildred Trotter worked) in 1951, and then taught pathology at the University of Virginia and Tufts

Illustration 4.3   **Thomas Jefferson and Sally Hemings**

DNA analysis proved that a Jefferson, but not necessarily
Thomas, had fathered children by the slave Sally Hemings, a
rumor going back to 1802.

University. Friends persuaded Foster that he should try to test the old ca-
nard about Jefferson with the new techniques of DNA fingerprinting.

Although Foster was intrigued, he knew little about the new techniques of DNA fingerprinting. DNA (deoxyribonucleic acid, a molecule
in the cell nucleus) had been discovered in 1869 and later proved to be
one of life's building blocks. In 1953 James Watson and Francis Crick
showed DNA to be a double-helix polymer combining the bases A, G,
C, and T. To solve crimes, forensics experts learned to cut DNA strands
with a restrictive enzyme, put fragments in a gel with electrodes, use
an electric current to sort DNA fragments by length, and produce x-ray
photos known as autoradiographs. These displayed the visual bands that
could compare DNA profiles of different individuals, as in the case of
the Romanovs and Prince Philip.

To carry out the tests, Foster lined up a team of geneticists at Alec
Jeffreys's laboratory in Leicester, England, to help him. Foster found it

relatively easy to obtain blood samples from the descendants of Eston Hemings and Thomas Woodson, two of Sally Hemings's sons, along with various Jeffersons in the area. Since Thomas Jefferson's sons produced no male offspring, there was no surviving male line to study. But Foster was able to get samples from the male descendants of Field Jefferson, Thomas's maternal uncle.

When the Leicester scientists found that descendants of Eston Hemings and Field Jefferson had the same set of y-chromosomes in their DNA, the case that Thomas Jefferson could have been Eston Hemings's father strengthened. When Foster suggested the case for paternity, the media picked up the story.

The article's headline "Jefferson Fathered Slave's Last Child" hardly suggested the cautious and complex conclusions of the article that appeared in *Nature* on November 5, 1998. What Foster and his Leicester team reported was simply that someone with male Jefferson y-chromosomal DNA—not necessarily Thomas—was probably the father of Eston Hemings. The *Nature* article also found that tests results from six descendants of three of Thomas Woodson's sons showed that Thomas Jefferson could *not* have been the father of Thomas Woodson. But the article, appearing during the impeachment proceedings against President Bill Clinton for perjury regarding his sexual misconduct, fell on fertile ground.

The scientists had no Thomas Jefferson DNA to analyze. Their protocols were designed simply to see if *any* male Jefferson might have fathered Eston. Yet Joseph Ellis, a Jefferson biographer and historian facing charges of lying to his classroom students at Mount Holyoke College about his own past, announced in his own article in that same issue of *Nature* that the DNA evidence "seems to seal the case that Jefferson was Eston Hemings's father." But it showed no such thing, and Ellis joined Trevor-Roper among the distinguished historians who have jumped to conclusions about forensic matters they barely understood and got completely wrong.

In private, Foster backed away from the conclusion that Thomas Jefferson fathered Eston Hemings. In an e-mail he sent to Professor Robert F. Turner on October 1, 2000, Foster stated only that "the DNA tests do tell us that Eston Hemings was very likely fathered by a member of the Jefferson family." It was "possible" that that member could have been Thomas Jefferson. But two days later, in another e-mail, Foster wrote "there is nothing in [our] DNA study that itself would lead [us] to suspect Thomas Jefferson as the father versus Randolph [Jefferson, a brother] or his sons." The DNA tests showed only that it was *possible* that Thomas Jefferson was the father of a child by Sally Hemings—nothing more.

In April 2001, a Scholars Commission on the Jefferson-Hemings Matter reported that the allegation that Thomas Jefferson fathered a child by Sally Hemings was "by no means proven." In 1800 there were many male Jeffersons living within twenty miles or so of Monticello. Many were frequent visitors at Jefferson's home. Many had fathered children by their slaves. DNA testing could not distinguish among two dozen adult male Jeffersons. At least seven of them—including Thomas—were at Monticello when Eston was conceived, a statement based on historical, not forensic, evidence. All that Foster's 1998 tests showed was that "a descendent of one of Sally Hemings' children carries Jefferson genetic markers." But which Jefferson was the father?

The Jefferson-Hemings case showed the risks of jumping to conclusions about the new DNA testing for identity. A retired pathologist with little knowledge of genetics or DNA conducted an experiment that produced results much more tentative than reported in the press. A historian and biographer of Jefferson jumped to conclusions as well. Public opinion rushed to judgment that a former U.S. president had fathered a child by one of his slaves. But forensics showed no such thing, only that Jefferson was among those family members who *might* or *could* have had relations with Sally Hemings. Indeed, the tests showed that Thomas Jefferson was not the father of Thomas Woodson, one of Sally's children. The story of Jefferson's paternity was too good to be true. Once again, the media transformed forensic history from scientific caution into exaggeration and speculation.

4.4 Jean-Jaccques Cassiman: The Heart of the Last King of France

About the time that Anna Manahan in Virginia was being unmasked as a pretender who claimed to be Anastasia, daughter of the last tsar of Russia, European geneticists were working on another pretender story involving Louis XVII, the ten-year-old last king of France. Louis-Charles, Duc de Normandie, was the son of King Louis XVI and his wife, Marie Antoinette, who were executed in 1793 during the Reign of Terror in the French Revolution. Louis-Charles reportedly died in the Temple prison tower in Paris in 1795. Some believed he may have escaped and wandered the United States as the "lost dauphin," made famous in Mark Twain's *Huckleberry Finn* as "the dolphin." There were hundreds of pretenders claiming the identity and inheritance of the dead dauphin. The question was: where was the body of Louis XVII?

During his incarceration, many countries indeed recognized the imprisoned child as the new king. There was therefore great consternation and suspicion when he died in prison on June 10, 1795. The death certificate read: "Register of the decease of Louis-Charles Capet, on the 20 Prairal at three o'clock p.m., aged ten years and two months, native of Versailles, residing at Paris in the Temple tower, son of Louis Capet, last king of the French, and of Marie-Antoinette-Josephe-Jeanne of Austria." Within hours of his death, the child king was buried in a common grave. But his doctor, Philippe-Jean Pellatan, removed the boy's heart and preserved it, so that the heart ultimately ended up as a mummified relic in a crystal urn at the Abbey of Saint-Denis in Paris.

For years, numerous pretenders appeared claiming to be King Louis XVII, claiming to have escaped his jailers and to be roaming the earth in search of his inheritance and perhaps his throne. Eleazar Williams, half Native American, turned up as a claimant in New York in the 1820s. The swindler Baron de Richemont, another pretender claiming to be the French king died in 1853. The Prussian clockmaker Karl Wilhelm Naundorff filed his claim in Leipzig in 1831. When he died in Delft, Holland, in 1845, the Dutch government duly buried him as the legitimate French king.

The dauphin's heart was even more mysterious. Somehow it vanished from Dr. Pellatan's desk drawer in his Paris home at Rue de Tourraine. By then, it was immersed in vinegar and had become hard and solid. The heart turned out to have been stolen by Pellatan's assistant, one Jean-Henri Tillos, and later returned to the doctor by Tillos's father. In May 1828, Pellatan, by then eighty-one years old, donated the royal heart to the archbishop of Paris, who kept it hidden away behind the books in his library.

The rest of the dauphin's body was exhumed in June 1894 from the Sainte-Marguerite Cemetery in Paris and produced the expected pile of bones, skull, teeth, and hair for scientists to examine. But the heart was, quite naturally, missing.

After World War II, investigators exhumed the body of Karl Naundorff in Delft. They tested the humerus (upper arm bone) for arsenic, thinking the real king might have been poisoned, but found only trace amounts. Nor did his hair under a microscope match the hair of the dauphin recovered from the Paris cemetery. In 1954, a French court, tired of decades of squabbling over the fate of the dauphin, declared that he had indeed died in prison in 1795. There the matter rested. Case closed—they thought.

After Alec Jeffreys developed the techniques of DNA fingerprinting in 1985, scientists began to take a new look at the case of King Louis XVII. Jean-Jacques Cassiman, a geneticist working at University Hospital in Leuven, Belgium, was surprised in 1992 to receive a telephone call from a Dutch historian, Hans Petrie, asking if he would be willing to test some hair related to the case of the missing dauphin. The hair belonged to Karl Naundorff and had been exhumed in 1950. Cassiman agreed.

In fact, Cassiman, jumped at the chance. "It was a scientific challenge," he wrote. "We wanted to be able to show whether the Prussian clockmaker was Louis XVII or not." During the autumn of 1992, Cassiman began to compare the mtDNA from Marie-Antoinette's hair with that from Naumdorff. He used PCR (polymerase chain reaction) technology to amplify the DNA and isolated the D loop of 1,100 base pairs of mtDNA from Naumdorff. He then obtained hair from Marie-Antoinette and her two sisters from a rosary stored at a convent in Klagenfurt, Austria. In March 1995, Cassiman traveled to Klagenfurt and examined the medallions of hair preserved from each of Marie-Antoinette's sixteen children.

By 1998 Cassiman was able to publish his results in the *European Journal of Human Genetics*. His test results showed that Naundorff's bone and hair samples of mtDNA had two nucleotides different from the sequence in the hair of Marie-Antoinette and her two sisters. The samples also differed from those of four living maternal relatives descended from Marie-Antoinette. Cassiman concluded that it was "unlikely" that Naumdorff was the son of Marie-Antoinette.

But how about the heart of Louis XVII? In 1998 Cassiman received a telephone call from another historian, Philippe Delorme, in Paris, saying that Delorme could obtain a piece of Louis's heart for analysis if Cassiman had any interest. The by now thoroughly desiccated and hardened heart had traveled from a chateau in France during World War II to Madrid, then back to France in 1975. The heart was now lodged in a crystal urn in the Memorial at Sainte-Denis, a private cemetery for French royalty. The Duc de Bauffremont, director of the Memorial, kept the heart in an underground chapel at the Basilica in the cemetery. He agreed to allow Cassiman to test its content.

In June 1999, Cassiman saw the heart for the first time and agreed to examine some samples. Bernard Brinkman, another geneticist at the University of Münster in Germany, agreed to conduct independent tests as a control. Neither the Belgian nor the German had any particular passion for the outcome of tests on the heart of a dead French king. On December 15, 1999, the heart was solemnly transported by hearse to Thierry Cote Medical Laboratory not far from the cemetery at Sainte-Denis. Here doctors carefully sawed off the tip of the heart and gave pieces to Cassiman at Leuven (500 mg) and Brinkman at Münster. The heart samples then went into freezers that also contained hair samples from Marie-Antoinette and her two sisters.

The two scientists ground the heart pieces to dust and placed them in sterile tubes with enzymes that helped separate out the mtDNA. They then placed the DNA in a PCR machine capable of making millions of copies and selected three identical sequences of mtDNA for study. "As soon as we had the little boy," wrote Cassiman, "we could see his sequence was identical to the living relatives [four descendants of Marie Antoinette]." In fact, they discovered an exact match. But was there also a match with the DNA from Marie Antoinette and her two sisters?

Using new probes, Cassiman reduced his DNA samples to small, 100 to 200 base-pair fragments that would make the tests more accurate. A single hair from Marie-Antoinette's sister Johanna-Gabriela turned out to be a perfect match with the samples from Louis XVII. On April 3, 2000, Cassiman and Brinkman met and concluded that they had obtained identical results. "Not only did we have sequence alignment and identity from the heart with living and deceased relatives," stated Cassiman, "but we also had independent confirmation from another laboratory."

The media were fascinated, as was understandable. On April 19, 2000, Cassiman, Brinkman, and the Duc de Bauffremont held a press conference in Paris to announce their results before the assembled reporters and television cameramen. Cassiman was measured and cautious. "The scientific tests," he announced, "can only show that the heart in the crypt has to belong to the son of a maternal relative of the Habsburg family." But he was more certain in his response to queries from reporters. "Yes, I'm satisfied. If you take our results with the historical evidence—and if that is correct—then, our results are one hundred percent. Everything

Illustration 4.4   **Louis XVII's Heart**

The well-traveled heart of King Louis XVII in its crystal urn at Sainte-Denis.

seems to indicate that it was the young dauphin who died alone in the Temple prison in tragic circumstances." The press loved it. "The results of the mtDNA analysis of the heart at the Center for Human Genetics (Leuven) and at the laboratory in Münster show that the heart mtDNA D-loop sequence and the sequence of maternal relatives of Louis XVII are identical," concluded Cassiman in his announcement.

Cassiman's tests seemed to put an end to more than two centuries of mystery, pretense, and fascination with the fate of Louis XVII. The scientific results seemed definitive. The boy king did die in prison in Paris in 1795. The many pretenders were false. But forensics had not so much revised history as combined forensic with historical evidence to produce a more complete and sensible conclusion. The heart of the "lost dauphin" could finally in 2004 return to the crypt at Sainte-Denis and rest in peace, thanks to the conclusions of modern forensic science—and forensic history.

4.5 Linda Strausbaugh: Hitler's Skull

A fragment of a skull exhibited in Moscow in 2000 showed two bullet holes and was alleged to be that of Adolf Hitler. In 2009 Connecticut state archaeologist Nick Bellantoni examined the skull, retrieved bone and blood samples, and had geneticist Linda Strausbaugh run DNA tests. She concluded that it was the skull of a woman about forty years old but not necessarily Eva Braun, Hitler's wife. Hitler's remains, it turned out, had been taken by the Red Army and Soviet intelligence from Berlin to Magdeburg, Germany, in 1946, buried, and then disinterred, burned, and the ashes scattered on KGB orders in 1970. The Moscow skull featured two bullet holes from entry and exit wounds, but was not Hitler's. Nor was there any chain of evidence linking the skull to Berlin in 1945. Once again, DNA tests produced a dead end, not a famous skull. But they also closed a case.

In the bombed-out ruins of Berlin, at about 3:30 in the afternoon of April 30, 1945, Adolf Hitler and his wife, Eva Braun, reportedly committed suicide. Within an hour, their bodies were burned and buried in a bomb crater. The next day Joseph Goebbels, his wife Magda, and their six children also perished in a suicide-murder arrangement. On May 2, Red Army troops entered Hitler's underground bunker. Two days later, they found the two corpses of Hitler and Braun in the bomb crater and reburied them. On May 5, Soviet intelligence officers exhumed the two bodies and in June moved them contained in wooden boxes to Ratenow, east of Berlin, where they were buried for the third time.

On November 1, 1945, British MI6 officer and historian Hugh Trevor-Roper announced at a press conference in Berlin that Hitler was indeed dead, having shot himself, and that Eva Braun had poisoned herself with cyanide capsules. Trevor-Roper's report was significant because rumors were rife that Hitler was still alive and had escaped the carnage in Berlin. Was the Führer somehow alive and well in Norway, Spain, Switzerland, Holland, or South America? By May 1947, Trevor-Roper's MI6 report had become a book titled *The Last Days of Hitler*. The book was an overnight sensation that seemed to put to rest the idea that Hitler had escaped and was alive somewhere. But a book did not constitute the bones. Hitler's body was still missing. "These bones," admitted Trevor-Roper in his book, "have never been found." So where was Hitler's body?

In September 1945, the Soviet government had issued an official statement that "no trace of the bodies of Hitler or Eva Braun had been discovered." The statement was a lie.

On February 23, 1946, Soviet intelligence officers from the Third Army section of SMERSH ("Smert shpionam!" or literally "Death to spies!") unearthed a pit in the Ratenow forest east of Berlin and removed the remains of Hitler, Braun, and Joseph and Magda Goebbels and their six children. They carefully packed the bodies in wooden boxes and moved them to the city of Magdeburg in what was now East Germany, or the German Democratic Republic. There they were examined that spring by a Soviet commission headed by forensic pathologist Pyotr Semenovsky. One skull, apparently Hitler's, was that of a male and contained a bullet hole. After examination, the remains were buried for the fourth time in a courtyard. There they would lie until 1970.

In 1968, as Czechoslovakia tried to break free of Soviet domination during its "Prague Spring," a Soviet book reopened the case of Hitler's missing remains. Lev Bezymenski had served in the Red Army in Berlin in 1945. Now he published his book, *The Death of Adolf Hitler*, in West Germany, then London and New York. In it he quoted the account of Soviet intelligence officer Ivan Klimenko regarding Hitler's body. The bodies of Hitler, Eva Braun, and their two dogs were allegedly placed in blankets, then boxes, and taken to the headquarters of Third Army intelligence in the Berlin suburb of Buch. Here an autopsy showed that Hitler's body was that of a male between fifty and sixty years old who stood 165 centimeters tall, both accurate numbers. The skull consisted of an occipital bone, left temporal bone, lower cheekbone, and upper and lower jaws. The teeth and bridgework matched the records and description by Hitler's dental technician. There was only one testicle (as with Hitler). And there was no bullet hole. Was Hitler poisoned? The plot thickened.

On March 26, 1970, the head of the KGB in Moscow, Yuri Andropov, launched a top-secret "Operation Archive." The bodies of Hitler and his party were yet again exhumed and examined. Then, sometime after April 4, they were burned on a bonfire near Schonebeck, about seven miles from Magdeburg. KGB officers dumped the ashes into the Biederitz River. Surely now Hitler was gone forever.

But that was not to be the case. In 1972 Reidar Sognnaes, a researcher at the UCLA School of Medicine in Los Angeles, California, discovered five x-ray plates of Adolf Hitler's teeth taken in 1944. Somehow they found their way to California after the war. The plates matched the dental features in Bezymenski's book perfectly. So Hitler's jaw and teeth seemed to have been authentic. But where was his skull?

Twenty years later the Soviet Union had collapsed, but doubts remained about what had happened to Hitler's remains. Only a few people in the KGB knew the real story of Andropov's "Operation Archive." Then, during the summer of 1992, journalist Ada Petrova paid a visit to Anatolii Prokapenko, director of the State Special Trophy Archive in Moscow. Petrova was investigating the death of Stalin in 1953. But in the course of their conversation, she learned from Prokapenko that Hitler's skull was "right here in Moscow," as the director put it.

With Prokapenko's assistance, Petrova discovered a remarkable Hitler Archive in the Russian Federation State Archive in Moscow. The "Operation Myth File" contained a number of papers and artifacts under the title "Hitler and His Entourage, I-g-23." Petrova quickly learned that there had been two, not one, Soviet commissions investigating Hitler's death in Berlin in 1945. Within the year she and her co-author Peter Watson had published their findings in a book titled *The Death of Hitler*. Here the authors described the "Operation Myth" search to find Hitler's remains, and a skull with a hole in it that forensic scientist Victor Ziagin claimed—with 80 percent certainty—belonged to Adolf Hitler.

In 1993 Moscow announced that Russia had Hitler's skull in custody. Werner Maser, a distinguished German historian, promptly declared that the skull was a fake. Nevertheless, in April 2000, the Federal Archives Service exhibit called "The Agony of the Third Reich," celebrating the fifty-fifth anniversary of the Soviet victory over Nazi Germany, showed the skull with its two bullet holes. In July, Yakov Pogony, the head of the archives of the Russian security police (FSB, formerly the KGB), pronounced that "the jaw is the main piece of evidence, and the main piece of evidence must be preserved." But another archives official, Alexander Kalganov, countered, "I have not seen any documents providing evidence that this is the skull of Hitler."

In September 2005, Hitler's disputed skull was still in Moscow. A team of forensic scientists in Rome published an article on Hitler in

Illustration 4.5   **Hitler's Skull?**

The media announced Hitler's death in 1945. But
where was the body? And did the Russians have his
skull in Moscow?

which they concluded that "the skull bone fragment with a gunshot
wound possibly from Hitler's corpse has not been properly examined."
They went on to propose a new test. "It might be useful to re-examine
the skull fragments, to study their integrity, to compare them with the
data from the autopsy of 1945, and to obtain samples for mitochondrial
DNA (mtDNA) analysis." Once again, pathology was giving way to
DNA fingerprinting to find proof of identity.

In 2009 Dr. Nick Bellantoni, a forensic anthropologist and archaeologist associated with the University of Connecticut at Storrs,
became interested in the Hitler skull in Moscow. Bellantoni was the
Connecticut state archaeologist and a very popular adjunct teacher
of anthropology at the university. Bellantoni flew to Moscow, spent

an hour examining the skull, and then used cotton swabs to get some DNA samples. He then flew back to Connecticut and tested the skull DNA at the university's Center for Applied Genetics, directed by Linda Strausbaugh. Strausbaugh had received her PhD from Wesleyan University and had taught in the Department of Molecular and Cell Biology at UConn since 1980. At Storrs she and Bellantoni worked on the skull with two of Michael Baden's protégés from the medical examiner's office in New York, Craig O'Connor and Heather Nelson. Both were former UConn students.

Strausbaugh and her American team immediately discovered that the skull DNA samples had not been archived or stored properly. For three days, they used molecular copying techniques to replicate the skull DNA. "We were very lucky to get a reading," noted Strausbaugh, despite the limited amount of genetic information. The results were stunning.

"We know the skull corresponds to a woman between the ages of twenty and forty," announced Bellantoni. "The bone seems very thin, male bone tends to be more robust. And the sutures where the skull plates come together seemed to correspond to someone under forty." Bellantoni also had procured photographs taken by the Red Army of Hitler's sofa in the bunker in 1945. That sofa was now in Moscow and Bellantoni had taken blood samples from the sofa wood and fabric. "I knew I was working with the real thing," he said. The skull DNA did not match the bloodstain DNA from the sofa. The young woman's skull with the two bullet holes did not belong to Adolf Hitler.

But the Russians were not convinced. In December 2009, Vasily Khristoforov of the FSB complained that "these researchers never got in contact with us. With what could they have compared the DNA?" Khristoforov did not know that Bellantoni had taken home samples of DNA not only from the skull, but from Hitler's sofa as well. Then the Russians backed off. "No one claimed," said Vladimir Kozlov of the Russian State Archive, "that was Hitler's skull." They had, of course, but it wasn't.

By 2009 historians had long been convinced that Hitler and Eva Braun had both died in the bunker in Berlin in 1945. Their remains had been cremated and thrown into an East German river in 1970. Reports of Hitler's bones and skulls seemed completely spurious. As Christopher Browning, an American historian of Nazi Germany noted regarding the historical evidence and interpretation of Hitler's death, "None of it is depending on the alleged validity of a body or skull in Russian possession."

Pathology, DNA fingerprinting, and historical evidence all confirmed that the skull in Moscow did not belong to Adolf Hitler. The Russians had the autopsy photographs and Hitler's remains were long gone. But the media were less interested in the science or the forensic history than in the Hitler skull story.

References

4.1 On Clyde Snow and the unearthing of Mengele's remains, see Christopher Joyce and Eric Stover, *Witnesses from the Grave: The Stories Bones Tell* (Boston: Little, Brown, 1991). The best single account of the Mengele hunt and DNA analysis is by John Conroy, "On the Trail of Josef Mengele," http://m.chicagoreader.com/chicago/on-the-trail-of-josef-mengele.

For a brief but solid online biography of anthropologist Clyde Snow, see http://digital.library.okstate.edu/encyclopedia/entries/S//SN001.html.

4.2 The first account of finding the Romanov remains was by Robert Massie, *The Romanovs: The Final Chapter* (New York: Random House, 1995). See also Greg King and Penny Wilson, *The Fate of the Romanovs* (Hoboken, NJ: John Wiley, 2003), which includes direct communications from Michael Baden and William Maples. On the Romanov DNA, see Peter Gill et al., "Identification of the Remains of the Romanov Family by DNA Analysis," *Nature Genetics* 6 (1994): 130–135, and more recently, Evgeny L. Rogaev et al., "Genomic Identification in the Historical Case of the Nicholas II Royal Family," *Proceedings of the National Academy of Sciences* 106, no. 13 (March 31, 2009), 5258–5263, and Michael D. Coble et al., "Mystery Solved: The Identification of the Two Missing Romanov Children Using DNA Analysis," *PLOS ONE* 4, no. 3 (March 2009): 1–9.

4.3 On Eugene Foster and the controversy over Sally Hemings and the Jefferson DNA, see Robert F. Turner, ed., *The Jefferson-Hemings Controversy: Report of the Scholars Commission* (Durham, NC: Carolina Academic Press, 2011). Foster overstated the case in his original "Jefferson Fathered Slave's Last Child," *Nature* 396 (6706) in 1998. On the new technique of DNA fingerprinting, see the biography of Alec Jeffreys at http://en.wikipedia.org/wikiAlec_Jeffreys (2011).

4.4 The story of J.J. Cassiman and the king of France's DNA is told by Deborah Cadbury, *The Last King of France* (London: St. Martin's Press, 2002). For the technical discussion, see J.J. Cassiman et al., "Mitochondrial DNA Analysis of the Putative Heart of Louis XVII, Son of Louis XVI and Marie-

Antoinette," *European Journal of Human Genetics* 9 (2001): 185–190. Cassiman announced his results in a press conference on April 19, 2000: www.chez.com/louis17/english.html.

4.5 On the dispute over Hitler's alleged skull, see Ada Petrova and Peter Watson, *The Death of Hitler: The Full Story with New Evidence from Secret Russian Archives* (New York: W.W. Norton, 1995). A more recent article on Hitler is Daniela Marchetti et al., "The Death of Adolf Hitler: Forensic Aspects," *Journal of Forensic Science* 50, no. 5 (September 2005), Paper ID JFS 2004314.

Not-So-Cold Cases

The public wanted its cases closed, not open. People were less interested in historical truth or modern science than in ending ambiguity and having a mystery solved and concluded. The media—especially television and the Internet—fed the public appetite for novelty by transforming every forensic revision of the past into a sensational and global virtual reality within hours or even seconds.

Belief trumped inquiry. People really wanted to believe that a conspiracy killed John F. Kennedy or Zachary Taylor, that Anastasia was still alive, that Jefferson fathered children by his own slave, or that the skull in Moscow was Adolf Hitler's. When the initial and often inaccurate reports of ballistics, atomic evidence, or DNA fingerprinting proved to be untrue, the public ignored the science and moved on to another sensation.

By the twenty-first century, virtual reality took over. Television viewers saw the horror of 9/11 in real time as the twin towers of the World Trade Center descended into dust, death, and fire. The final hunt to kill Osama bin Laden appeared on television and websites worldwide, with President Obama and his team hunched over their own television feed watching the final moments of vigilante justice and a state-sponsored revenge murder. CSI programs multiplied until every city in the United States seemed to have an earnest team of detectives flying everywhere to solve crimes while young, brilliant laboratory technicians tracked criminals by computer and examined forensic evidence. The line between historical reality and scientific truth, on the one hand, and appealing fictions, on the other, became a postmodern blur.

The media and the public tried constantly to co-opt the forensic scientists and get them to make extraordinary claims on camera as soon as possible. Journalists had in the past urged scientists to confirm that more than one shooter tried to kill Kennedy, that Josef Mengele was indeed the real Josef Mengele, and that the "Hitler Diaries" were authentic, not a forgery. The media pressured scientists into going public with their findings before they had been published and subject to peer review, as in the cases of the virus that caused the 1918 flu or the possibility that King Tut of Egypt had been murdered by his prime minister Ay 3,300 years ago. The comedian Stephen Colbert interviewed a scientist on his television show and poked fun at her findings regarding the rivets on the *Titanic* as a cause of the ship's sinking. Journalists embellished the story of computer hacker Kevin Mitnick and the Japanese-American who tracked him down with cyberforensics, the hacker versus the samurai. "Catch me if you can!"

The nature of both history and forensic science is to keep cases open, not closed. History is subject to a continuous process of review and revision in an argument without end, as one historian put it. Innocent men and women have gone to jail for years, only to have their convictions overturned by DNA evidence or new testimony not available at the time of their trial. Cold case files and databases may still be reopened and reexamined as long as the evidence is maintained intact. But by the time a case is reopened and a decision in court is reversed, the public has often forgotten or lost interest in what happened. Historians and forensic scientists, on the other hand, persist in their quest for the truth. Past crimes may be forgotten, but their solution is never entirely abandoned. The investigators keep chugging along.

5.1 Jeffrey Taubenberger: Tracking the Killer Virus of 1918

The crime was mass murder, a pandemic that killed between 50 and 100 million people worldwide between September 1918 and the summer of 1919, far more victims than perished during World War I. The killer was a virus. But which virus did it? The murder mystery involved numerous suspects, but was unsolved until the twenty-first century. Nobody knew precisely why millions had died at the hands of this killer.

The influenza epidemic of 1918–1919 killed 675,000 Americans, more than perished in two world wars, Korea, and Vietnam. People choked to death within days on the fluid in their lungs, often as a result of the pneumonia that followed the flu. Baseball players, streetcar conductors, and ordinary citizens donned gauze masks as a protective measure.

The flu seemed to have some resemblance to the medieval Black Death or the Siberian flu epidemic of 1889. Later scientists tried to link it to swine flu or bird flu. But the 1918 flu was different, and nobody knew how or why it was so deadly, killed so many healthy young adults, or vanished so swiftly.

The first full account of the flu by a historian was Alfred Crosby's *America's Forgotten Pandemic*, which appeared only in 1989, then was reprinted in 2003. Crosby, an American studies professor at the University of Texas, Austin, provided an extensive account of the flu's devastating path across the United States, Samoa, and Alaska. He provided tables of mortality statistics to show that most victims were young adults, the same age cohort as had fought in the war. He showed the effects of the flu on big cities and small towns. But the historian was stumped by the question of causation: what kind of flu virus was it and how did it spread so rapidly and kill so many people? Historians could not answer such a question, but virologists and forensic pathologists could—if they could obtain a living flu virus and apply the techniques of modern DNA analysis.

Jeffrey Taubenberger was a forty-eight-year-old virologist working in Washington, DC, when he read Crosby's book. Taubenberger was born in Germany where his German father worked for the U.S. Army. When his father was transferred to the Pentagon in 1970, young Jeffrey began a career in science that led to an MD and PhD at the University of Virginia Medical School in 1987, then to a career in pathology at the National Institutes of Health and the National Cancer Institute. Taubenberger soon became a talented young researcher—precise, meticulous, and cautious. Instead of a lab coat, he wore slacks and shirts, and in his spare time enjoyed his hobby of playing woodwind instruments and composing music.

In 1993 the Armed Forces Institute of Pathology (AFIP) invited Taubenberger to start up a new laboratory in molecular pathology. He promptly set up shop at the Walter Reed Medical Center in a windowless five-story concrete building constructed to resist a hydrogen bomb explosion. Taubenberger soon discovered that AFIP, founded by President Abraham Lincoln during the Civil War, had a warehouse repository that housed hundreds of thousands of tissue samples collected over more than a century. The tissues were typically fixed in formaldehyde and set in small paraffin wax blocks. "We keep everything," Taubenberger remarked—"clinical histories, glass slides, paraffin blocks."

Illustration 5.1   **The Flu Virus of 1918–1919**

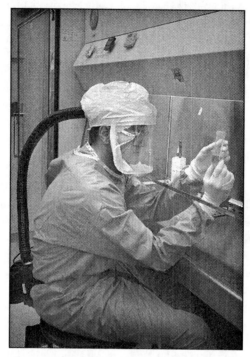

The flu epidemic of 1918–1919 killed tens of millions of people worldwide, but no one knew the genetic makeup of the virus that caused it.

One of Taubenberger's assistants, Amy Krafft, had succeeding in isolating the morbillivirus RNA from dolphin tissues using the modern technique of polymerase chain reaction (PCR). The scientists wondered if they might apply similar techniques to a flu virus from 1918. They soon found that their warehouse held seventy-seven wax blocks of tissue taken from the bodies of American soldiers who died during the epidemic. Most important, seven of these had died quickly from the initial viral infection, and not from the subsequent pneumonia that ravaged their lungs.

The flu genome had some 13,000 base pairs of adenine, quanine, cytosine, and uracil, and seemed to belong to the H1N1 subtype of the flu virus. Amy Krafft on July 23, 1996, identified the 1957 flu virus and determined to test the 1918 variant. She and Taubenberger used the tissues of two American soldiers that exhibited living viruses. Roscoe Vaughn had died on September 26, 1918, at Camp Jackson, South Carolina, and the virus was still living in the tissue of his right lung preserved in the warehouse. Nine fragments of viral RNA were isolated for study. By the summer of 1997, Krafft had the full sequence of hemagglutinin from Vaughn. Hemagglutinin, discovered in 1941, is a protein distinctive in flu viruses that makes red blood cells clump together, resulting in a red button at the bottom of a test tube. In September, Krafft got more tissue from James Downs, another American soldier who had died of the flu at Camp Upton, New York, in 1918.

In 1996 Taubenberger's lab had submitted papers to *Science* and *Nature*, both prestigious journals. The papers were rejected without even being sent out for peer review. When the scientists finally were able to publish their preliminary results in *Science* in March 1997, they were fortunate enough to have them read by another scientist on the West Coast, Johan Hultin. Hultin was virtually unknown to the scientists in Washington. But he now made a significant contribution to the puzzle of the killer virus.

Hultin was no amateur. Born in Sweden, he came to the United States in 1949 and began his study of microbiology at the University of Iowa, where he received a master's degree in 1952 and began to work on anthrax and bacteria related to the problems of biowarfare. In 1951 Hultin became interested in the 1918 flu virus and reasoned that living virus tissue could be obtained from a body frozen in permafrost. He decided to explore the Teller Mission in Brevig, Alaska, on the Seward Peninsula, where seventy-two out of eighty residents had died of the flu. Their bodies had been deeply buried in frozen ground for thirty-three years.

"This was a great adventure for a little boy from Sweden," Hultin later recalled. "I had never spoken to Eskimos before. I thought I was going to find the virus alive, I really did." He and his team of scientists received permission to exhume the victims, taking care to utilize sterilized instruments and surgical masks. But unfortunately the tissues from four bodies (lungs, kidneys, spleens, and brains) that Hultin examined produced no live viruses, and the project failed. Hultin went on to work in community hospitals in the San Francisco area in the 1950s and became an ardent alpinist and adventurer. He retired to Los Gatos, California, in 1988.

In 1997 Hultin was involved in putting the finishing touches on a Norwegian-style cabin in the mountains when Taubenberger telephoned him in response to a letter Hultin had written. Taubenberger had no idea that Hultin had gone hunting for the 1918 virus forty years earlier. Hultin offered to return to Alaska at his own expense ($3,200), which he did. He then shipped Taubenberger the tissues from the body of an obese woman in her twenties (nicknamed "Lucy") who had died of the flu in 1918. Lucy, like Roscoe Vaughn and James Downs, would make a vital contribution to modern medicine.

Taubenberger's laboratory was soon able to use PCR to fish out pieces of the 1918 virus and reconstruct its genetic code. Ann Reid, Taubenberger's assistant, cut thin slices of paraffin blocks, added xylene as a solvent, and produced free-floating tissue samples from Vaughn, Downs, and Lucy. When the gene fragments were spread out on a thin gel and subjected to an electric current, x-ray film showed dark bands in the fragments. The scientists finally had the evidence to crack the code of the virus.

In 1998 another scientist entered the scene. Kirsty Duncan was a thirty-one-year-old medical geographer from Toronto. She obtained a PhD in geography from the University of Edinburgh (1992), but had no training in virology. In fact, she taught climatology at the University of Windsor in Canada. But she was fascinated by the story of the 1918 flu epidemic. Like Taubenberger, she had read Crosby's history of the disaster. She knew nothing of Johan Hultin's pioneering search for the virus in Alaska. In 1994 she discovered the story of seven young Norwegian coal miners who had gone to the town of Longyearbyen on the island of Spitsbergen to seek work in 1918 and had promptly died of the flu. Their bodies had been quickly buried and rested ever since in permafrost.

After four years of preparation and ground surveys, Duncan launched a well-publicized scientific expedition to Norway in 1998 to exhume the bodies of the seven miners. By then she had met Taubenberger and was aware of his work. In September 1998, despite endless complications and funding problems, and only after a local pastor blessed the graves, Duncan's team unearthed the bodies. Taubenberger had initially been a member of the team, but then dropped out, believing that the chances of recovering viral RNA from the bodies were nonexistent because of the acidic environment.

A year later, Duncan's team in England was finally getting some results from tissue samples. Duncan knew by then that Taubenberger and Reid had sequenced three genes of the 1918 virus and that they considered the Spitsbergen expedition "showy." At a conference in London in November 1999, Duncan's group announced their findings to the media without prior publication—violating the normal means of subjecting new information to peer review. They also refused to share samples with Taubenberger. Duncan asserted that her data were different from those of Taubenberger and Reid and that the 1918 pandemic may have involved more than one virus. By 2002 Duncan had the samples in England and Canada, but she never published a paper on her results. She ultimately turned to politics and was elected a member of parliament in Canada in 2008. She told her story in *Hunting the 1918 Flu* in 2003 and remained bitter about her failure.

Meanwhile, Taubenberger continued his work. In 2005 he published in *Science* and *Nature* results establishing the structure of the 1918 flu genome. The work involved three laboratories: Taubenberger's at AFIP, the Southeast Poultry Research Laboratory, and the Mount Sinai School of Medicine in New York. They had successfully established the virus's genetic sequence. *Science* called it the "breakthrough of the year" in science. Taubenberger credited Johan Hultin for Hultin's discovery of Lucy in the Alaskan permafrost, which was the key to Taubenberger's research. The samples of Lucy's tissue were sizable and significant. "He pretty much took most of a whole lung," said Taubenberger.

The work continued, however. In 2007 scientists reported that monkeys infected with the re-created virus showed 1918-type symptoms and died of an overreaction of the immune system. In September 2008, scientists exhumed the body of one Mark Syes in Yorkshire, who died of the H5N1 bird flu and was buried in 1919 in a lead coffin. In 2009 scientists at the University of Wisconsin connected three specific genes (PA, PBI, and PB2) with a nucleoprotein from 1918 flu tissue samples and showed how the flu could invade the lungs and cause pneumonia. Then in June 2010, a Mount Sinai team showed that a 2009 H1N1 flu vaccine also provided some cross-protection against the 1918 flu virus.

Identifying the genetic composition of the 1918 flu virus provided for the first time a scientific explanation of the causes and virulence of the epidemic. Historians could trace the effects and count the mortality rates, describe the quarantine measures and the terrible toll in lives. But without modern virology and genetics, they had no idea who the real killer was. Only forensic pathology and PCR studies of the tissue samples from long ago unearthed in the permafrost could achieve that goal. Historians had shown *how* the flu epidemic spread across America and around the world. Scientists had shown *why* the epidemic began in the first place and identified the virus that killed so many.

5.2 Tim Foecke and Jennifer McCarty: Testing the *Titanic* Rivets

In this case, the body in question was an ocean liner two miles beneath the surface of the North Atlantic. In 1985 undersea divers discovered the remains of the luxury liner *Titanic*, which sank off Newfoundland in 1912 after brushing up against an iceberg. Examining the remains of the ship, especially its rivets, with electron microscopic scans, modern metallurgists Tim Foecke and Jennifer McCarty placed at least some responsibility on the shipbuilders of Belfast who cut corners and utilized child labor to produce millions of faulty rivets, made of wrought iron, not steel, that were substandard and failed on impact.

Why exactly did the *Titanic* sink the way it did in two hours and forty minutes on its maiden voyage to New York? The ship's brush with an unexpected iceberg in the late evening hours of April 14, 1912, south of St. Johns, Newfoundland, created a tragedy of epic proportions. Two-thirds of the passengers and crew—some 1,500 people—perished. British and American inquiries agreed that the ship was traveling at about 22 knots per hour on impact and sank at 41° 46′ N, 50° 14′ W. The owner of the ship was the British-registered White Star Line. The builder was Harland and Wolff, which owned a massive Queen's Island shipyard complex in Belfast, Ireland. The *Titanic* was one of three monumental *Olympic*-class ships built for the trans-Atlantic trade in the optimistic era before World War I. Of the 1,317 passengers, 500 were saved and 817 lost at sea. Of the 891 crew members, 212 were saved and 679 were lost.

The ship struck an iceberg on the starboard side. Passengers and crew heard the sound of ripping, grinding, or brushing of metal against ice. There was no sudden impact of a collision, but the contact was sufficient to open up the first five watertight compartments of the hull in approximately seven seconds. Within slightly less than three hours, the great ship broke in half and sank to the bottom of the sea, a distance of more than two miles. Survivors rowed to safety in lifeboats or were picked up from the sea by the first ship to arrive, the *Carpathia*. For sixty years and more, the *Titanic* rested somewhere in the North Atlantic, but no one knew exactly where. Everyone blamed someone else for the disaster.

Subsequent investigation based on accounts of the survivors showed that the great ship had lifeboats capable of holding only half the number of passengers and crew, no lifeboat instruction, and officers who believed the ship was "unsinkable" and did little to expedite the evacuation of the ship until it was too late. The captain had minimized warnings of ice in the area, although he had changed course a few miles to the south. The ship was proceeding at nearly top speed (22 knots) despite warnings from other ships about ice. Wireless messages and distress signal rockets fired in the night were received by ships in the area, but only the *Carpathia* took decisive action to come to the aid of the *Titanic*. By then it was too late.

On September 1, 1985, a joint U.S.-French expedition led by Robert Ballard and Jean-Louis Michel finally discovered the wreck and debris field of the *Titanic* some 4,000 meters (2.5 miles) deep in the North Atlantic. Ballard had worked as an oceanographer at the Woods Hole Oceanographic Institute, founded in 1930 in southern Massachusetts opposite Martha's Vineyard. Ballard worked on deep-sea dives with a submersible nicknamed *Alvin*. He began thinking about the *Titanic* in 1973 and a year later received his PhD in marine geology. After finally locating the wreck, Ballard and Michel returned a year later in the summer of 1986 and explored and photographed the wreck and debris field with the help of *Alvin* and a portable camera known as *Jason*. They took thousands of photographs. But after five dives, they failed to see the expected 300-foot gash in the side of the hull on its starboard side. They did, however, see the steel plates of the hull broken apart at their riveted seams. The riveted plates had separated. Why?

The subsequent 1987 expedition began salvage operations, bringing up some 1,800 artifacts from the ship's wreck. Over the next few years there would be both legal and illegal dives to retrieve artifacts. In October 1994, the first exhibit of 150 objects recovered from the *Titanic* was held at the National Maritime Museum in London, titled "The Wreck of the *Titanic*."

Two years later, two American metallurgists became interested in studying the wreck. Tim Foecke received his PhD in materials science from the University of Minnesota and was a specialist on how metals fracture under stress. In 1991 Foecke became a staff scientist at the National Institute of Standards and Technology (NIST) in Gaithersburg, Maryland. A decade later, he began teaching failure analysis and forensic studies as an adjunct professor at Johns Hopkins University

Illustration 5.2 **The *Titanic* Rivets**

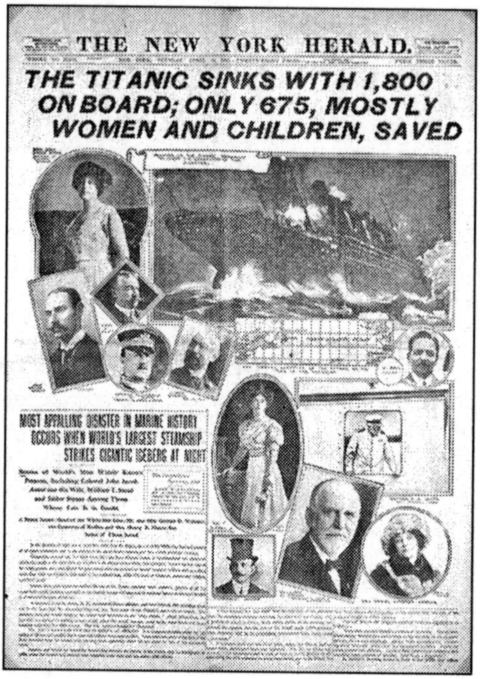
THE NEW YORK HERALD.

THE TITANIC SINKS WITH 1,800 ON BOARD; ONLY 675, MOSTLY WOMEN AND CHILDREN, SAVED

MOST APPALLING DISASTER IN MARINE HISTORY OCCURS WHEN WORLD'S LARGEST STEAMSHIP STRIKES GIGANTIC ICEBERG AT NIGHT

The "unsinkable" ship *Titanic* scraped against an iceberg and sank off Newfoundland during the night of April 14–15, 1912. Were substandard hull rivets a factor?

in Baltimore. In time, Foecke would study the metals of the battleship USS *Arizona*, sunk by the Japanese at Pearl Harbor, the Confederate submarine CSS *Hunley*, and the World Trade Center, as well as the *Titanic*. In 1998 Foecke originated the theory that the rivets on the ship's hull plates might be the culprit.

At Johns Hopkins, Foecke supervised a graduate student named Jennifer Hooper McCarty, who shared his interest in the *Titanic*. McCarty, a graduate of Temple University, had received her PhD in materials and scientific engineering from Johns Hopkins, was a specialist in historical materials, and worked at Oxford University on wrought iron and steel structures using rail materials in the National Railway Museum at York. She also studied archaeology and Bronze Age pottery in Greece. Her dissertation was on the metallurgy of the *Titanic*'s rivets.

The *Titanic*'s hull was constructed of thirty-foot by six-foot steel plates, an inch or more thick, overlapped and fastened together by 3 million rivets. The hull was double-bottomed and amidships was double- or even triple-riveted. Some rivets were made of steel, an alloy of iron and carbon. More commonly, they were made of wrought iron, although the red-hot "puddling" process left trace elements of slag in the iron. (Slag was iron silicate, a combination of iron, oxygen, and silicon.) By 1900 shipbuilders had increasingly used steel, rather than wrought iron, rivets. The *Titanic*'s contract called for steel rivets for most of the ship, but "iron rivets elsewhere." To ensure a watertight seal, rivets had to be driven in hot and could not be left loose or crooked.

By 1900 shipbuilders usually used hydraulic hammers, not human labor, to pound in the rivets to the hull plates. In the Belfast shipyard where the *Titanic* was being built, often the hydraulic hammers could not reach portions of the hull so rivet teams of five men and boys would do the final work. By 1912 there were 17,275 workers employed at the shipyard. The furious pace of shipbuilding meant that skilled labor was in short supply. Country farm boys became rivet boys overnight. Inexperienced rivet boys as young as thirteen had the crucial job of hand-hammering the iron rivets, especially the double rivets on the outer shell of the hull.

There were a number of causes of faulty rivets on the great ship. There were hundreds of work-related accidents during the construction project. There was a lack of skilled riveters. Indeed, fewer than 60 percent of Harland and Wolff's labor force could be called skilled. Company records for 1911–1912 are full of complaints about the shortage of skilled riveters. The watertight seal between the hull plates was often weak. The modern discovery of the *Titanic*'s wreck would show in the end that there was no expected 300-foot gash along the side of the ship, and no evidence of fractured brittle steel. There were, however, broken rivets.

In 1991 tests by the Canadian Defence Research Establishment Atlantic (DREA) of the ship's steel suggested that perhaps hull steel in ice water could become brittle, especially if it contained too much sulfur. Naval architects in 1995 confirmed the conclusion of British investigators in 1912 that no more than 12.6 square feet of exposed hull had enabled the flooding of the first five compartments in the hull.

Five years later Tim Foecke used electron micrographs to show that the steel exhibited no brittle weaknesses. Then in 1997 he tested two rivets and found that they contained 9 percent slag—triple the normal amount.

In time, three more salvage expeditions (1996, 1998, and 2004) recovered thousands of objects from the wreck and produced tens of thousands of photographs. The Society of Naval Architects and Marine Engineers forensics panel utilized sonar imaging and subbottom profiling to identify not one but six opening slits along the starboard hull and 11.4 square feet of open space. In the summer of 1996, Paul Matthias of Polaris Imaging used subbottom profilers to photograph the bottom of the starboard hull and found slits running six, sixteen, thirty-three, and forty-five feet, fewer than 100 feet in total. The *Titanic* was hardly a weak ship. Among the objects recovered were forty-eight rivets. Some were broken, some intact.

The National Oceanic and Atmospheric Administration gradually took over the supervision of all salvage and exploration expeditions. In 1997 Tim Foecke had enough wrought-iron rivets to perform an analysis using an optical microscope and 46,000 digital images from the seabed. He discovered that the average value of slag in a rivet was four times the normally expected concentration, resulting in lower tensile strength. Computer models using finite element analysis (FEA) showed that wrought-iron rivets were five times more likely to fail under a given load than steel rivets. There were ruinous chunks of brittle slag within the rivets.

On December 19, 1997, Hollywood released *Titanic*, the highest-grossing film of all time until *Avatar* in 2010. Leonardo DiCaprio and Kate Winslet starred in a tragic love story of the fated voyage. A mockup of the ship was constructed in Mexico. For two years, a crew filmed the wreck. Researchers examined previously unknown archives and blueprints at Harland and Wolff. Everyone knew the story and the ending, but the film was a sensation.

Much less well known, but more significant, was Tim Foecke's technical paper "Metallurgy of the RMS Titanic," which came out in 1998. Foecke's tests showed that brittle steel was still a "possible" explanation for the hull damage, but that the rivets might well hold the key. Perhaps, concluded Foecke, "the microstructure of the rivets that evolved during their being driven into place, with the slag stringers oriented perpendicular to the tensile axis," had contributed to the disaster. At least the rivets need "further investigation."

That investigation took another decade. Together, Foecke and Mc-Carty toiled over the "rivet theory" in their laboratories and researched every angle of the problem. McCarty completed her dissertation on the rivets and went to work for the Oregon Health and Science University in 2005 in the Office of Technology Research and Collaboration. In 2008 they published their results as a book titled *What Really Sank the* Titanic. They concluded that the "brittle steel" theory was wrong. Rather, the wrought-iron feedstock supplied to Harland and Wolff was not of the highest quality for rivets and had been worked too little at the wrong temperature. This resulted in a distribution of different seam strengths along the hull with riveted joints of varying strength. The substandard rivets were not detectable by the methods of the day, but they had too much slag and were weakened.

The scraping of the *Titanic*'s hull against the iceberg was an unusual event that stressed the inadequate rivets. The damage to the starboard bow was significant. The riveted joints turned out not to be fail-safe. But some rivets would have failed anyway under the stress. Better quality feedstock would have meant fewer open seams and thus fewer flooded compartments. The *Titanic* might well have stayed afloat long enough for rescue ships like the *Carpathia* to arrive and rescue more passengers.

Tim Foecke explained the situation to reporters at a press conference in April 2008: "You need the slag but you need just a little to take up the load that is applied so the iron doesn't stretch. The iron becomes weak the more the slag there is because the brittleness of the slag takes over and it breaks easily." Broken rivets meant open rivet joints at the hull seams and water in the compartments. They meant the ship was doomed in the event of the wrong kind of collision.

Jennifer McCarty participated in a hilarious interview on the Colbert Report shortly thereafter, when Stephen Colbert asked her if the real cause of the *Titanic* sinking was either God or too many poor passengers below decks. McCarty survived Colbert's humor and was able to offer her own summary of her findings: "What likely happened was that when the iceberg hit key points along the side of the ship, the impact wasn't that strong, but it was enough to pop certain rivets that were holding these steel plates together," she said. "It wasn't one big gash, but lots of little holes. Water started to seep into the compartments, and in a short time, they started to fill."

Only in 2010 was the entire debris field of the *Titanic* mapped for the first time. The debris covered the ocean bottom over a three-mile by five-mile rectangle. Autonomous underwater vehicles (AUVs) conducted sonar imaging and took some 100,000 photographs of the area, now under the custody of RMS *Titanic* Inc., the legal custodian of the wreck. The robots moved around the debris field at about three miles per hour to get images with side-scan sonar devices. These images were then combined on a computer to create a forensic tool for mapping the debris field for the very first time.

Two years later, in April 2012, Guernsey's Auctioneers and Brokers of New York City announced an auction of 5,000 artifacts (jewelry, furniture, ship fittings, etc.) from the *Titanic* to be sold as a single lot. (A court had ruled that the collection had to be kept intact and remain open to the public for viewing.) The collection had been appraised in 2007 at $189 million. No one knew what to expect. After critics accused the auction organizers of being "grave robbers," the auction was postponed indefinitely.

Applying the tools of modern forensics and metallurgy to the historical question of why the *Titanic* sank the way it did in the time that it did was a crucial breakthrough. Foecke and McCarty discovered a technically significant cause—substandard rivets—that offered a new explanation of an old problem. Forensic tools helped revise historical understanding of a tragic and well-known disaster. They discovered a hidden cause of a multicausal disaster created by men's sense of their own infallibility in the domination of nature. Rivets failed. Nature won.

5.3 Zahi Hawass: The CT Scans of King Tutankhamun

Did somebody kill King Tut? Historians knew that the boy king Tutankhamun was the eleventh pharaoh of the Eighteenth Dynasty, that he ruled Egypt from 1336 to 1327 BCE, and that he died at the age of eighteen. Tutankhamun's body had been mummified and hidden for more than three millennia. Only in 1922 did a British team discover and open his tomb in the Valley of the Kings. And only in the 1960s did modern forensics open up the possibility that he might be a victim of homicide.

Tutankhamun's father Akhenaten had ruled Egypt for years under the official religion of Aten, a form of monotheism. But when Tutankhamun became king of Egypt, he quickly restored the polytheist religion of the Amun priests. The very name *Tutkenkhamen* meant "the living image of God, Amun." Egyptian society was deeply divided and at war with the neighboring Hittites. Tutankhamun depended considerably on the services of his prime minister (or vizier) Ay, a public official of great power whom he had inherited from his father. When Tutankhamun died young, Ay not only arranged his funeral and burial, but inherited the office of king and married Tutankhamun's widow. Ay had much to gain from Tutankhamun's death. But did he kill Tut?

In 1922 a British team of archaeologists headed by Howard Carter and financed by Lord Carnarvon descended upon the Valley of the Kings and discovered the tomb of Tutankhamun. In February 1923, they opened the tomb and found room after room of buried treasure and household goods, along with the mummified remains of the dead ruler. Carter at age fifty had long experience excavating the ruins of ancient Egypt. Since 1899 he had served as inspector general of antiquities for the Egyptian government. In 1925 he even got permission to perform an autopsy on the body of Tutankhamun. Carter's autopsy showed that the king was between five feet five inches and five feet eight inches tall, that his upper cervical vertebrae were fused (suggesting to some that he died of Klippel Feil syndrome, a bone disease), and that he had been glued to the coffin after being embalmed. But not much more would be known until the 1960s.

In 1968 Professor R.G. Harrison of the University of Liverpool, a well-known anatomist and expert on mummies, received permission from the government of Egypt to take the first x-rays of the body of Tutankhamun. In order to do, Harrison had to saw the body in half—it was glued to the coffin. Photographs of the head showed an area of density at the base of the skull. Might it be the result of a blow to the head from behind?

Harrison appeared on British television to describe his findings, but never published his results in the medical literature for peer review. In December 1971, however, he did publish an essay in the journal *Buried History* in which he concluded that his x-rays showed a "small piece of bone in the left side of the skull cavity." This could mean, wrote Harrison, that "Tutankhamun died from a brain hemorrhage caused by a blow to his skull from a blunt instrument." This speculative remark by Harrison would soon unleash the gods of controversy and open a murder investigation by experts and amateurs alike.

Controversy persisted for another twenty-eight years. In 1998 Bob Brier, a well-known and popular professor of Egyptology and paleo-pathology at Long Island University—known to his students as "Mr. Mummy"—took Harrison's x-rays of Tutankhamun to Dr. Gerald

Erwin, the head of radiology at Winthrop University. Erwin agreed that the x-rays indicated that Tut *might* have suffered a hematoma at the lower base of his skull, and that a blow to the back of his head *probably* caused the hematoma. Then Brier discovered that Tutankhamun's widow Ankhesenpaatan had married his successor Ay, making the case for homicide against Ay even stronger. Brier published his speculations as *The Murder of Tut: A True Story*.

A year later, in 1999, Zahi Hawass, director of the Supreme Council of Antiquities and the leading archaeologist in Egypt, discovered the Valley of the Golden Mummies, yet another complex of tombs that held the remains and possessions of more than 200 members of the Egyptian royal family. For several seasons he and his team combed the site for new discoveries. Hawass was a widely respected authority with a PhD from the University of Pennsylvania who had taught at UCLA and Cairo University. The discovery of new mummies heightened interest in the fate of Tutankhamun and reopened the question of whether he was murdered.

In 2001 two Utah state police officers, Mike King and Greg Cooper, began to investigate Tutankhamun's death as a possible homicide. Neither had any training in archaeology or Egyptology, but they consulted the experts. They visited Tut's tomb in the Valley of the Kings, flew over the site in a hot air balloon, and photographed his remains. They used modern police logic and forensic techniques to test the "reasonable suspicion" that Tut was a murder victim. They consulted British Egyptologist Joann Fletcher about the history of Tut and his period. Could modern forensics solve a 3,300-year-old murder? King and Cooper thought so, and in 2002 they announced their findings that Tutankhamun's successor Ay had the motive, opportunity, and means to commit the crime.

At about the same time, a facial reconstruction expert in London, Robin Richards, used Harrison's x-ray photographs and Gerasimov's techniques to create a digital skull of Tutankhamun, then facial tissue layers, and finally a clay mould of Tut's head, cast in fiberglass and then painted.

By then medical doctors were speculating that Tutankhamun might have died from a variety of diseases: Klippel Feil syndrome, a fusion of cervical vertebrae that was consistent with the x-rays of Tut; sickle cell disease, as proposed by two physicians in Hamburg, Germany; Marfan syndrome, suggested by Paul Doherty, a British historian; or a

Illustration 5.3   **Zahi Hawass**

Zahi Hawass, director of the Supreme Council of Antiquities and the most prominent archaeologist in Egypt, did not buy into the theories regarding the death of the pharaoh Tutankhamun. Was the pharaoh murdered by his prime minister?

tumor, as Christine El Mahdy, an Egyptologist, concluded, might have caused Tut's demise.

Dr. Richard Boyer, a doctor at Primary Children's Medical Center in Salt Lake City, Utah, examined Harrison's x-rays and concluded that Tutankhamun's body exhibited abnormal curvature of the spine and fusions of the upper vertebrae. It was "not a nice healthy looking cervical spine," he told an interviewer. "If he fell backward or there was a blow to the back of his head, a serious spinal injury at that level could be fatal." But was there any such blow? Certainly the work by Bob Brier and the two Utah detectives suggested that there was and that Ay delivered it.

In 2003 Boyer published his results in a peer-reviewed journal, the *American Journal of Neuroradiology*. "Our critical review of the skull and cervical spine radiographs of Tutankhamun," he wrote, "does not support proposed theories of a traumatic or homicidal death." The Utah policemen were disappointed.

Hawass had been most hospitable to King and Cooper, showing them around the Valley of the Kings and permitting them to examine Tut's tomb. But he too was not convinced that Tutankhamun was murdered. By 2005 he headed an Egyptian team utilizing modern forensic techniques—CT scans (computerized tomography) and DNA analysis—to reexamine Tut's death and the murder theories that were widely publicized. A CT scan of Tutankhamun in January 2005 showed thinning of the occipital bone that seemed perfectly normal. There was "no evidence of injury occurring before death to the cervical spine or the cranial-cervical junction." Nor did Hawass and his team find any evidence of a "depressed skull fracture, a posterior fossa subdural hematoma, or an injury to or congenital malformation of the cervical spine."

Hawass was not buying the murder theories. "The cause of death of the famous young pharaoh remains enigmatic, but the radiographs of his skull cannot be used to support a theory of homicide," he concluded. After all the speculation, the facial reconstruction, and the radiographs and CT scans, it looked like Tutankhamun had died a natural death.

DNA analysis was more specific. Between 2007 and 2009, Hawass and his team took DNA samples from the bone tissue of eleven royal mummies of the Eighteenth Dynasty, including Tut. They discovered that mummies KV55 and KV35YL, as they labeled them, were Tut's mother and father, much as DNA confirmed the pedigree and identity of the Romanov family. Thanks to genetics, Hawass was able to confirm a five-generation pedigree leading to Tutankhamun. Hawass concluded that the king probably died of avascular necrosis, a disease in which the bone tissue dies from lack of blood, and from malaria.

In 2010 the results of Hawass's DNA analysis were published in the *Journal of the American Medical Association*. The results of the 2007–2009 DNA studies of tissue from eleven royal mummies suggested neither murder nor Marfan's syndrome. The ancestry and pathology of Tutankhamun's family, examined with the techniques of modern forensics, again pointed to death by avascular necrosis and malaria.

Again, forensic science disappointed public opinion. King and Cooper had reissued their book in 2006 and criticized the careful conclusions of Hawass and his Egyptian team regarding the death of Tut. But the genetic evidence was increasingly ruling out murder and pointing to disease as the cause. A discovery that Ay had murdered Tutankhamun would have been a significant revision of history. A conspiracy surrounding the death of a ruler—Tutankhamun or President Zachary Taylor—had great appeal. Yet again conspiracy theory was contradicted by the much more prosaic explanations of forensics.

5.4 The U.S. Navy SEALs: Identifying Osama bin Laden

Sometimes the media devour a delicious forensic story that has no evidence at all to support it. On May 2, 2011, at about two o'clock in the morning local time, Osama bin Laden, the terrorist mastermind behind the 9/11 bombing of the World Trade Center in 2001 and other attacks in the West, was shot and killed by U.S. Navy SEALs at his secret compound in Abbottabad, Pakistan. The SEALs flew in helicopters (two Black Hawks and three Chinooks) from Jalalabad, Afghanistan, into Pakistan on a successful mission to kill bin Laden that took under three hours and evaded Pakistani air defense. According to the U.S. government, after facial recognition and DNA tests confirmed bin Laden's identity, the body was buried at sea in an "undisclosed location."

But how exactly did DNA testing prove that the dead man in Pakistan was in fact bin Laden? The most tantalizing story that went viral on the Internet in the days following bin Laden's death was that his DNA matched that of a sister who died in Boston of a brain tumor in 2005, whose tissues were subpoenaed by the FBI, and whose brain was on file in an FBI laboratory somewhere.

It was a fabulous forensic story. The only problem was that no one could find any evidence to support it.

The operation to kill or capture bin Laden had many years of preparation and surveillance behind it. Code-named "Operation Neptune Spear," it was conducted on direct orders from the president of the United States, Barack Obama, arranged by the Central Intelligence Agency, and carried out by a group of Navy special operations SEALs (from Sea, Air and Land) known as DEVARU/SEAL Team 6. The nighttime helicopter raid on bin Laden's secret compound in Abbottabad was launched from Jalalabad, Afghanistan, and watched in real time in the White House Situation Room by Obama and his national security team. Millions of television viewers saw the drama unfold. Within hours, the president announced that bin Laden was dead, that his body had been taken to Bagram Air Force Base in Afghanistan, then to the aircraft carrier USS *Carl Vinson* by V-22 Osprey helicopter, and finally dumped in the ocean.

It turned out that bin Laden's body had already been measured in Jalalabad and was some six feet four inches in length, precisely bin Laden's known height. In the airplane on the way to Jalabad, lacking a tape measure, one of the SEALs simply lay down beside the body to get an approximation of the dead man's height. The story quickly became a Washington joke, and four days later President Obama received a commemorative plaque with a tape measure mounted upon it.

Using facial recognition software (shades of Gerasimov), photographs of bin Laden's head and face were sent digitally to CIA headquarters at Langley, Virginia, and superimposed over existing photographs of bin Laden from the past. A SEAL photograph of bin Laden's face was uploaded to a server and sent to Washington. An eight-point facial recognition analysis led the CIA to conclude, "The length of his nose, the distance between his upper eye-lid and his lower eyebrow, the shape of the ear, cartilage—they all match." CIA director Leon Panetta informed President Obama that the match had 90–95 percent accuracy. In addition, women in the Abbottabad compound had identified bin Laden by name, and bone marrow and swab samples of his DNA were taken for analysis. The actual photographs of the body have not been released, nor are we ever likely to see them.

Michael Leiter, head of the national Counter Terrorism Center, knew he was looking at a dead bin Laden and remembers thinking, "I don't need facial recognition. It's Bin Laden with a hole in his head—immediately recognizable. Holy Shit! We just killed Bin Laden." But was it scientifically certain?

The official announcements on May 2, U.S. time, of bin Laden's death were carefully worded. The president's announcement at 11:35 p.m. the night before had said only that "after a firefight, they [the SEALs] killed Osama Bin Laden and took custody of his body." There was no mention of DNA or other issues around the identification of the body. The Department of Defense later in the day said only that "DNA analysis conducted separately by DOD and CIA laboratories has positively identified Osama Bin Laden. DNA samples collected from his body were compared to a comprehensive DNA profile derived from Bin Laden's large extended family. Based on that analysis, the DNA is unquestionably his."

The SEALs had extracted tissue from bin Laden's body in Abbottabad and placed samples in two sets of vials. One set went back to Jalalabad with bin Laden's body in a Chinook helicopter to be analyzed there. That sample was analyzed at Bagram Air Force Base, and the data was then sent electronically to Washington. The second sample was hand-carried by plane to the capital for another opinion.

Shortly thereafter, John Brennan, assistant to the president for homeland security, asserted that "now we can say with 99.9 percent confidence that this was Bin Laden." That was better than the 95 percent confidence of facial recognition.

But how had the government obtained DNA evidence from other members of the bin Laden family? From which family members did they obtain such evidence? And how could a match have been established so quickly? The public wanted to know.

Journalist Katie Moisse of ABC News probably started the virus by writing on the day bin Laden was killed that "it is unclear whether Bin Laden's sister, who died of brain cancer in Boston in 2005, was one of the relatives used in the comparison." Whether or not there even was a sister (unnamed) who died of brain cancer in Boston in 2005 was unclear, but this did not stop the media from weaving a colorful forensic history out of whole cloth.

The story went viral on the Internet within minutes. Hundreds of variants appeared on line worldwide. It became "the story that would not quit." And it got better in the telling. According to the story, the Navy SEALs had flown to Abbottabad with samples of bin Laden's DNA provided by the FBI from its brain bank, samples taken from the brain of his (still unnamed) sister after she died of brain cancer at Massachusetts General Hospital in 2005. In fact, CIA officers simply compared bin Laden's DNA with that obtained from other family members not identified.

The story mushroomed even after Sue McGreavey, public relations officer at Massachusetts General stated that the hospital had received many requests for information, but could not "turn up any evidence" that a bin Laden relative was ever in the hospital or that the FBI had ever requested access to bin Laden remains. The FBI office in Boston could not put a stop to the story. Special Agent Greg Comcowich said that he could neither confirm nor deny it. The public image of FBI agents secretly storing the blood and tissues of public enemies for future forensic use in a manhunt was simply too good not to be true. And it produced fabulous one-liners in cyberspace.

In truth, the bin Laden family was extensive and many brothers and sisters (not to mention nieces and nephews) of Osama bin Laden did in fact reside in the United States before 9/11. Osama's father Mohamed bin Laden (1905?–1967) was a sybaritic businessman who built the largest construction company in Saudi Arabia after World War II. By the time his son Osama came along, the Mohamed bin Laden Organization was a profitable family business that had million-dollar contracts

Illustration 5.4 **Osama bin Laden**

Family DNA and facial reconstruction confirmed that the dead man in Abbottabad was Osama bin Laden, the world's most wanted terrorist. Was there ever a dead sister in Boston?

with the Saudi government and other companies throughout the Middle East. Mohamed's DNA was widely distributed and available through his fifty-four children by various wives—twenty-five sons, including Osama, and twenty-nine daughters. Osama's mother Alia was Syrian and had given birth to Osama when she was fifteen. The bin Laden family was very wealthy, but no one knew precisely what that meant in terms of assets, holdings, and money.

The bin Laden children of Mohamed ranged in age over two decades, having been born between the end of World War II and 1967, when the patriarch died. Although concentrated in the Middle East, by the 1990s many had moved to the United States. Osama's brother Abdullah was the guardian of bin Laden family and business matters in New England and spent eight years at Harvard Law School in Cambridge, Massachusetts, before he finally received his law degree. Osama's half-brother Mohamed lived in New England. So did his half-sister Sanaa. Another half-sister, Khalita, traveled on a U.S. visa and lived in New England. By 2001 Osama bin Laden had perhaps twenty relatives living in or near Boston, most of whom flew home to Saudi Arabia under FBI custody within a few days of their estranged brother's attack on the World Trade Center in New York.

The FBI was quick to interview every bin Laden it could find in 2001 and afterward. The family had long declared themselves estranged from their most famous terrorist member, and the FBI found no evidence of complicity in the September attack. The FBI did, however, compile a substantial record of testimony, reports, and files on the family focused on the money traffic around the world. FBI agents managed to talk with both Abdullah and Mohamed in Boston and discovered that Harvard University had received $2 million from another brother, Bakr.

In July 2011, another story circulated that the CIA had organized a fake hepatitis B vaccination program in Abbottabad in 2010 in order to get DNA samples from bin Laden children living in the compound. Starting that spring, posters appeared in Abbottabad urging parents to vaccinate their children free of charge. Bribes were paid. There was mention again of the nameless sister who had "recently" died in Boston and whose brain provided a DNA sample of the bin Laden family identity. A Pakistani physician, Shakil Afridi, helped organize the bogus vaccination campaign. A Pakistani court consequently sentenced him to thirty-three years in prison for treason. In any event, the vaccination campaign failed to obtain the desired DNA from the bin Laden children.

Then, on September 23, 2011, federal judge Lewis Kaplan dismissed all the 1998 charges against the dead al-Qaeda leader related to a 1983 ambush of U.S. soldiers in Somalia, the bombing of two U.S. embassies in 1998, and the bombing of the USS *Cole* in Yemen. There were no charges pending against bin Laden for his most heinous crime, the attack on the World Trade Center in New York. In connection with the hearing, assistant district attorney George Toscas signed a statement that bin Laden's DNA had been compared in Afghanistan with a "comprehensive DNA profile derived from multiple members of Bin Laden's family." The government had "high confidence" that the dead man was in fact Osama bin Laden. And there was no mention of a dead sister in Boston.

The story of the dead sister and her brain appears to have been a media concoction, not forensic history. The sister had no name. Massachusetts General Hospital had no record of a bin Laden dying there in 2005 or any other time. The FBI had made no requests to subpoena the remains of a dead woman at the hospital.

The truth was that bin Laden did have two half-sisters who had lived in Boston, that the U.S. government claimed to have a DNA profile of the bin Laden family, and that the FBI's Boston office had interviewed bin Laden relatives in the area and compiled files on their financial dealings.

What would a forensic historian need as evidence to confirm or deny the story of Osama bin Laden's dead sister? Certainly a death certificate would be needed to show the date, time, and place of death, not to mention the name and identity of the sister. Then we would need hospital records of any brain, blood, or tissue samples taken to provide DNA for analysis. In addition, the FBI would have to provide records of any subpoena or attempt to retrieve DNA from the hospital. We would want to see the DNA results of both bin Laden and his other family members to be compared for a match. We would like the Navy SEAL records of the disposition of bin Laden's body, from Abbottabad to the seabed, including records of the taking of samples from the body for analysis. We would want to see the photographs—however gruesome—of the dead man's face that were provided for facial recognition analysis in the United States.

Many requests have been made for such evidence. Nothing has been forthcoming. There are no scientific journal articles that might be subjected to peer review. There are hundreds of articles, blogs, and tweets on May 2, 2011, and virtually nothing of substance afterward. It is entirely likely that the wonderful story of bin Laden's Boston sister and her brain stemmed from a media feeding frenzy that immediately followed the death of Osama bin Laden. The story went viral on the Internet and then disappeared into cyberspace. We will probably never know if, or how, bin Laden's sister—whatever her name, if she existed—played any role in the identification of the world's leading terrorist. She was a great forensic story, but not part of forensic history.

In May 2012, California treasure hunter Bill Warren claimed he had located bin Laden's body 200 miles west of the Indian city of Suret on the ocean floor of the Indian Ocean, not the Arabian Sea. (He had searched a year earlier, but found nothing.) If Warren locates bin Laden's body, he plans to conduct DNA tests to establish his identity. Sound familiar?

5.5 Tsutomu Shimomura: Catching Kevin Mitnick

Cyberforensics is the science of tracking, identifying, and apprehending hackers in cyberspace who may have committed cybercrimes. These terms are all problematic. Only recently have laws emerged defining what exactly criminal behavior means with respect to computers. Cyberforensics too has developed as a field of study only in the past two decades. Much of the field deals with obtaining computer evidence related to noncomputer crimes, such as rape or murder. But increasingly it deals with cybercrimes committed *on* the computer or over the Internet, such as hacking, the unwanted intrusion into another person's computer. The crimes and the detective work all occur in cyberspace. And hackers range from teenagers who get thrills from intruding into the networked computers of others to malicious "malware" creators who set loose worms, viruses, and logic bombs in cyberspace that can penetrate and destroy hardware and software connections to the Internet worldwide. They threaten computer users everywhere.

Hacking into computers emerged with the appearance of the personal computer in the mid-1980s at about the time that DNA first became a tool for authenticating personal identity and "fingerprinting" individuals. Hacking began as a series of teenage pranks on the telephone that utilized the con of "social engineering"; that is, impersonating another individual over the telephone in order to obtain information. The divestiture of the Bell Telephone Company and the profusion of new telephone companies provided fertile new ground for hackers. With the growth of wireless networks of computers and the vast cyberspace of the Internet, hacking became a global nuisance and spawned the threat of anarchist destruction in every single computer worldwide.

Hacking is an ambiguous art and source of innovation in computing. The hacker is an intruder and a trespasser, but may or may not be a thief. Hackers may steal or may simply observe or copy information. Hackers flourish worldwide and are both a threat to, and a potential weapon of, nation-states. They may simply be joyriders having fun in cyberspace (a word first coined in 1982), going online wherever they can out of curiosity. Or they may be real threats whose computer hacking evokes our primal fears of insecurity and vulnerability.

In 2011, at the time that the decade-long search to find and kill Osama bin Laden concluded, renowned computer hacker Kevin Mitnick told his incredible story of cybercrime and his flight from the law in his book *Ghost in the Wires*. Mitnick began hacking into the telephone system in California in the 1980s just as personal computers and cell phones were coming into use. After decades on the run from the law and the government, Mitnick transformed himself from a "darkside hacker" into a computer security expert who could help companies and

Illustration 5.5   **Kevin Mitnick**

Hacker Kevin Mitnick became a media legend even
before he went to prison for allegedly committing
crimes with his computer.

governments prevent other hackers from intruding into their proprietary
or national security domains.

The story of how Kevin Mitnick broke into the computer of another
computer expert, Tsutomu Shimomura, and then fell victim to Shimomura's own skills of cyberforensics makes for fascinating forensic history. But it has also become the stuff of myth, legend, and a story that
goes far beyond historical truth.

Mitnick was born in 1963 in Van Nuys, California, into a family of
middle-class Jews from Eastern Europe. His parents divorced when he
was three, his mother remarried several times, and his stepfather abused
him. He grew up a hyperactive young man who hated authority and
took Ritalin and Dexadrine to control his loneliness, anger, and anxiety.
He began his career as a con artist by using Los Angeles bus system
transfers to obtain free rides. As a teenager, Mitnick became a "phone
phreak," hacking into the Pacific Bell Company's mainframe computer
in Los Angeles in 1981. He was eighteen. He continued his obsession
with hacking through all of his years at Monroe High School, Pierce
College, and the University of Southern California, from which he never
graduated. In 1988 he was arrested for hacking into the Digital Equip-

ment Corporation (DEC) to obtain its source code for VMS operating software. He was sentenced to twelve months in prison and three years of supervised release on parole, which he served.

Mitnick's actions ranged from pranks to crimes. Besides the DEC case, he was charged by the authorities with evading the FBI and hacking into the computers of Motorola, Nokia, Sun Microsystems, and Fujitsu Siemens. He allegedly read people's e-mail at MCI and DEC, wiretapped the California Department of Motor Vehicles, wiretapped National Security Agency (NSA) agents, and hacked into the computers of the FBI, the Pentagon, Novell, USC, and NORAD, the North American Aerospace Defense Command. Most of Mitnick's activities depended on the telephone system. There was as yet no wireless Internet world to explore and exploit.

Mitnick always maintained that he hacked out of curiosity and never stole property, harmed anyone, or destroyed files. "I was in the thrall of a power obsession," he wrote. "I didn't do it for the money," he added; "I did it for the entertainment." The journalist John Markoff created the myth of Kevin Mitnick as a "most wanted computer criminal" in articles in the *New York Times* that labeled Mitnick a "cyberthief" and a relentless hacker pursued by the FBI for his crimes. After his capture in 1995, a Los Angeles grand jury in September 1996 indicted Mitnick on twenty-five charges that included computer and wire fraud (copying proprietary source code), possessing the computer passwords of others, intercepting passwords, and damaging computers by inserting backdoors (a means of leaving and reentering a computer) into computers through his modem and the telephone network. The federal government alleged that Mitnick had caused $300 million worth of damages, a charge that Mitnick and his friends found ludicrous and vigorously denied.

In March 1999, after spending several years in prison without formal charges, Mitnick signed a plea agreement with a district court in California confessing to four counts of wire fraud, two counts of computer fraud, and one count of illegal interception of wire communication. The court sentenced him to forty-six months in prison and another twenty-two months for violating his parole, a total of sixty-eight months, more than five years. Since he had already served most of his sentence, Mitnick was released on January 21, 2003. He agreed not to profit from any films or books about his escapades for seven years, that is, until 2010. In 2011 he told his version of the story in his book *Ghost in the Wires*.

Whatever his agreement with the court, Mitnick was a media sensation after 1995. Markoff had already written a book about Mitnick in 1989 called *Cyberpunk*. People called him a threat to national security, a man who could start a nuclear war by whistling into a payphone to computers at NORAD. Tsutomu Shimomura wrote a book with Markoff in 1996 called *Takedown* about how he had run Mitnick to ground by computer sleuthing. The "Free Kevin" movement began in 1998 to get Mitnick out of jail. Mitnick himself published *The Art of Deception* in 2002, before he was silenced by the court, and went on to found Mitnick Security Consulting. On August 18, 2011, Mitnick conducted a hilarious interview on *The Colbert Report* with television host Stephen Colbert.

Mitnick's big mistake, it turned out, was to break into Shimomura's computer in December 1994, producing a two-month online war between the cyberthief and the Samurai, as the press called them. Mitnick later alleged that he broke into "Shimmy's" computer using a backdoor that he installed to obtain "root privileges" so that he could archive and compress everything that he wanted. But the forensic history of how the Samurai caught up with the cyberthief is far more interesting than that.

At the basis of cyberforensics is the notion that it takes a hacker to catch a hacker. The crime of hacking can be very complex. The evidence that will stand up in court is often tentative. The forensics of autopsying computer evidence can be even more complex. Hacking may or may not leave trace evidence, and the forensic historian needs sophisticated tools to find the traces. During a computer break-in, log files get shorter, not longer. Key evidence may consist of file modification times, the history buffer that stores information on all URL sites visited by an intruder or the user, and the time and duration of every log-on.

Today a wide variety of tools for cyberforensics is available on line. There are programs to crack passwords and show what the intruder knew. Files accessed can provide clues to motives. Berkeley Packet Filters installed in a computer while it is still running can be a powerful surveillance tool for re-creating an attack. There are computer tools (EnCase, FTK, and Coroner's Toolkit, which is designed for UNIX machines), tools for dealing with computer memory (Memoryze, Responder, and Second Look), tools for mobile devices (Cellebrite Mobile Forensics, Radio Tactics Aceso, Paraleben Device Seizure), and others (Hashkeeper, Evidence Eliminator, DECAF). None of these were available in 1994, however, and Shimomura's detective work would now be considered ancient forensic history.

But the evidence of computer forensics remains about the same: hard drives, software, CDs, peripherals (modem, cell phones, and manuals), fax pages, logs, passwords, backup disks, and all kinds of printed evidence. Tsutomu Shimomura was a pioneer forensic historian without really knowing it.

Shimomura, born in Nagasaki in 1963, came from a much more functional family than Mitnick. His father Osamu won the Nobel Prize in Chemistry in 2006 for his work on jellyfish bioluminescence, conducted mostly out of his laboratory at Woods Hole Oceanographic Institute in Massachusetts. Tsutomu grew up in Princeton, New Jersey, where his father taught for a time, and then attended Cal Tech in the 1980s, where his mentor was the brilliant prankster and physicist Richard Feynman, another Nobel Prize winner. Shimomura became deeply involved with computers, developing an uncanny ability to visualize what was happening in the new world of cyberspace. He worked for a time at the Los Alamos National Laboratory in New Mexico, then for Sun Microsystems in California in the 1990s.

When Shimomura realized his computer had been hacked in December 1994, he had no idea who the intruder was. Was it another phone phreak? What files and e-mails had been read, modified, or created? When? Shimomura promptly began to read the logs and make a chronology of the intruder's actions. He used a Berkeley Packet Filter to see the origin and destination of information. The filter could handle 100,000 packets of information per second. He identified stolen software programs. He discovered data file 0108.gz, a list of 20,000 credit card account numbers of Netcom subscribers. He utilized a program called Catch to backtrack through his files and organize data. After the FBI got involved, Shimomura used trap-and-trace tools of the telephone company and discovered that the culprit had used a so-called "gkremen" telephone account in Raleigh, North Carolina, leasing a network connection to Netcom.

The chase was complex. "In cyberspace," noted Shimomura later, "a vault can be stripped without any sign, at first glance anyway, that a theft has even occurred, for what is stolen is not the original piece of software or data, but a copy that the thief makes." Intruders may also erase trace evidence of their presence, comparable to wiping off fingerprints at a crime scene.

Within two months, the FBI and Shimomura had tracked Kevin Mitnick to an apartment complex in Raleigh using a Triggerfish RDF unit. On Valentine's Day 1995, they arrived with a warrant for his arrest. "How did you know it was Kevin who broke into your machine?" someone asked Shimomura later. "I didn't," he replied. "The things he was interested in on my computer were the kind of things Kevin would go after, but the attack was very sophisticated." Mitnick had chosen the wrong person to hack, and Shimomura had played forensic historian to bring him to ground.

By the time Mitnick had told his full story, in 2011, the public had found another computer hacker to mythologize. Bradley Manning, a troubled young gay U.S. Army private from Oklahoma, had obtained hundreds of thousands of unclassified and secret documents on the Iraq war between November 2009 and May 2010. These included several video versions of an American helicopter attack on Iraqi civilians in 2007 that Manning downloaded to his army workstation while serving in Iraq. Investigators discovered that Manning had downloaded and "streamlined" U.S. cables in order to move them out of his computer, allegedly to an organization of hackers led by an Australian, Julian Assange, who called themselves WikiLeaks. Like Mitnick, the WikiLeakers sought an open universe in cyberspace where secrecy and proprietary information were unknown. In fact, they had their own political agenda of embarrassing the United States and other great powers by exposing their evil acts.

The forensics experts who analyzed Manning's computer after he was caught, arrested, and brought to justice through a court martial proceeding came from the army's Computer Crime Investigation Unit (CCIU), located in Fort Belvoir, Virginia, and created in 1998. Special Agent David Shaver of the CCIU subjected Manning's computer workstation to a thorough autopsy. He found evidence that the username Bradley. manning was linked to all the files. More than 100 searches used the keywords "Julian Assange," "WikiLeaks," and "Iceland," especially on instant message logs between Manning and another hacker, Adrian Lamo. Shaver found over 100,000 U.S. State Department cables in an HTML zip file coded "blue" and listing 251,288 "message record identification numbers" in an Excel spread sheet.

Shaver also discovered that Manning had used a computer tool known as Wget, available on the Internet to download very large data files. Manning had no authority to do so. Wget was a program that retrieved data from web servers via HTTP protocols so they could be downloaded, converted into links for offline viewing, or supported by proxies. Wget had been a well-known tool since 1996. In particular, Manning had used Wget to download files quickly and easily from the Net Centric Diplomacy database at the State Department. Logs provided evidence that Manning had begun using Wget in March 2010. Shaver and his digital detectives and examiners (trained at the Department of Defense's Cyber Investigations Training Academys [DCITA]) had produced a virtual autopsy of Manning's cybercrimes that would serve as powerful evidence in a trial.

On the basis of Shaver's computer autopsy and other information, the army charged Manning with twenty-two separate indictments, including aiding the enemy. If convicted, soldier Manning might well face life in prison or even the death penalty.

Manning and Mitnick were very different types of computer criminals. Mitnick had enjoyed a decade-long joyride of curiosity, poking around in the computers of governments, corporations, and individuals primarily because he could do so. He was imprisoned for crimes that had barely been defined on computers that depended on the telephone system. There was as yet no Internet to hack and no wireless communications among computers in a global network.

Manning was allegedly a much more serious threat to national security, stealing classified and unclassified diplomatic and military information and passing it along to an organization hostile to American interests. The computer world had greatly changed between 1995 and 2010. Cyberspace provided a universe open to both cybercrime and cyberforensics. Hackers were members of a worldwide community, tolerated even by the regimes of Russia, China, and Iran in hopes that they could be a controlled weapon of cyberwar, not a threat to closed systems of government. Hacking was commonplace; cyberwar had already begun (as in Chinese penetrations of American computer technology or the alleged U.S. or Israeli Stuxnet attack on the Iranian nuclear centrifuges).

In any event, computers are now a standard body of evidence for criminal investigators, whether or not the crime has been committed using the computer. Like bones, blood, and DNA, hard drives and software programs can and do speak to the trained detective or examiner. Whether they knew it or not, computer experts like Shimomura and Shaver were forensic historians in search of a usable past whose evidence could stand up in court.

References

5.1 The best general history of the flu epidemic of 1918–1919 is Alfred W. Crosby, *America's Forgotten Pandemic: The Influenza of 1918* (Cambridge, UK: Cambridge University Press, 1989, reprinted 2003). On the pioneering work of Johan Hultin, see Elizabeth Fernandez, "The Virus Detective," *San Francisco Chronicle*, February 17, 2002. Journalist Gina Kolata tells the story of the scientific search for the flu virus by Jeffrey Taubenberger and others in *Flu: The Story of the Great Influenza Pandemic of 1918 and the Search for the Virus That Caused It* (New York: Simon & Schuster, 2005). Kirsty Duncan presents quite a different view of her own attempt to study the virus in Norway in her book *Hunting the 1918 Flu* (Toronto: University of Toronto Press, 2006). On the scientific discovery, see Jeffrey K. Taubenberger et al., "Initial Genetic Characterization of the 1918 'Spanish' Influenza Virus," *Science* 275, no. 5307 (1997): 1793–1796.

5.2 The best account of forensic testing of the metallurgy of the *Titanic*'s rivets is by Jennifer Hooper McCarty and Tim Foecke, *What Really Sank the Titanic?* (New York: Kensington, 2008). Foecke initiated the discussion with his paper "Metallurgy of the RMS *Titanic*" in 1998 for the National Institute of Standards and Technology, NIST-IR 6118. On the discovery of the wreck of the *Titanic*, see Robert D. Ballard, *The Discovery of the* Titanic (New York: Warner Books, 1987). A more recent centennial account of all aspects of the *Titanic* disaster is by Samuel Halpern et al., *Report into the Loss of the* SS Titanic: *A Centennial Reappraisal* (Stroud, Gloucestershire, UK: History Press, 2011). My visit to the new *Titanic* museum in Belfast, Northern Ireland, in June 2012 provided me with many insights into the famous disaster, including an exhibit of the five different types of rivets used on the ship and a demonstration of rivet boys installing the rivets.

5.3 On Zahi Hawass and King Tut, see the book by two detectives, Michael R. King and Gregory M. Cooper, *Who Killed King Tut? Using Modern Forensics to Solve a 3,000-Year-Old Mystery* (Amherst, NY: Prometheus Books, 2006), which makes the popular case for murder. The scientific literature includes Richard S. Boyer et al., "The Skull and Cervical Spine Radiographs of Tutankhamen: A Critical Appraisal," *American Journal of Neuroradiology* 33, no. 3 (2003): 1142–1147; Howard Merkel, "King Tutankhamen: Modern Medical Science and the Expanding Boundaries of Historical Inquiry," *Journal of the American Medical Association* 303, no. 7 (2010): 667–668; and Zahi Hawass et al., "Ancestry and Pathology in King Tutankhamun's Family," *Journal of the American Medical Association* 303, no. 7 (2010): 638–647, reporting on the 2007–2009 genetic studies of royal mummies. See also Zahi Hawass, *Secrets from the Sand: My Search for Egypt's Past* (New York: Harry N. Abrams, 2003). Hawass announced the results of the CT scan of Tut in a press release on March 8, 2005: http://guardians.net/hawass/press_release_tutenkhamun.

5.4 On bin Laden's family, see Steve Coll, *The Bin Ladens: An Arabian Family in the American Century* (New York: Penguin, 2008). The best account of the efforts to capture or kill bin Laden after 2001 is by Peter Bergen, *Manhunt: The Ten-Year Search for Bin Laden from 9/11 to Abbottabad* (New York: Crown, 2012).

5.5 Kevin Mitnick tells his story of hacking in his recent book with William Simon titled *Ghost in the Wires* (New York: Little, Brown, 2011). Earlier and more sensational journalist accounts are by Jeff Goodell, *The Cyberthief and the Samurai* (New York: Dell, 1996) and Tsutomu Shimomura with John Markoff, *Takedown* (New York: Hyperion, 1996). On cyberforensics tools and computer evidence, see Albert J. Marcella and Robert S. Greenfield, *Cyberforensics: A Field Manual for Collecting, Examining and Preserving Evidence of Computer Crimes* (Boca Raton, FL: CRC Press, 2002).

Conclusion

Modern Forensics and Historical Revision

For historians, the cases of the past are never really cold, or closed. The morgue and laboratory of history remain open, even when we think we know the end of the story. Both history and forensics always stand ready to revise their findings on the basis of new evidence. That evidence may well prove to be a matter of life or death, emancipating the innocent and convicting the guilty long after the fact. Forensic history may revise a long accepted conventional wisdom. Or it may confirm that wisdom.

In 1991 scientists unearthed Oetzi the Iceman, an early murder victim who died some 5,300 years ago in the Swiss Alps. Oetzi slept peacefully for millennia under many feet of ice. From his well-preserved remains and genome map, the scientists determined that Oetzi had brown eyes, Lyme disease, type-O blood, cavities, and tattoos. He was lactose-intolerant and enjoyed a last meal of ibex before being shot in the back by an arrow. In 2012 scientists used a minuscule atomic force microscope and light-scattering Raman spectroscopy to identify red blood cells preserved for 5,000 years. The protein fibrin confirmed that Oetzi died from his arrow wound. You can be dead a very long time and still leave lots of evidence behind that speaks to forensic historians.

In investigating the crime scenes of history, forensic historians are always open to new knowledge. Like detectives or medical examiners, forensic historians try to discover the truth based on the available evidence. Evidence and interpretation lead them to create narrative and argument. Historians want to tell a good (and true) story that makes a convincing point. They may end up by revising, or confirming, the conventional wisdom. Or they may fill a gap in our knowledge with new information.

Illustration 6.1   **Oetzi the Iceman**

A Vienna museum reconstruction of Oetzi the
Iceman, a 5,000-year-old homicide victim, based
on modern forensics.

To autopsy the body in question, forensic historians depend upon
expert help in obtaining and analyzing the evidence. For bones, they
need to consult a pathologist. For a skull, they can use facial reconstruction experts. Blood samples and DNA provide valuable data for the
geneticist. Hair can yield atomic evidence to be tested by physicists in a
nuclear reactor. Rusted rivets require a metallurgist or two. A computer
autopsy means finding a computer expert. And if the crime is forgery,
rather than murder, they probably need to consult a chemist or document examiner.

Modern forensic science has significantly affected historical debate
over some well-known past crimes or mysteries, utilizing modern
DNA, nuclear, and chemical analyses to reexamine the past. Many
forensic scientists have worked together over the years on historically
significant cases. The House Select Committee on Assassinations in

the 1970s investigated the murders of John F. Kennedy, Robert F. Kennedy, and Martin Luther King. In doing so, it created forensic teams of men and women who would later work together in the 1980s and 1990s on the cases of Zachary Taylor, Josef Mengele, and the Romanovs, for example. They became forensic historians, as well as pathologists and geneticists.

These men and women were trained as forensic pathologists, immersed in the bones, teeth, and blood of numerous victims of wars, murders, and airline crashes. After the discovery of DNA fingerprinting in 1985 in England, they learned that the clinching evidence in many cases would be genetic rather than pathological. Not that pathology is obsolete. It is not. Pathology remains essential to forensic work. But for a forensic historian, the last word in identification today is more likely to be a DNA match than a dental x-ray or a bone measurement.

Most historical research, of course, does not involve forensics at all. Historians comb the archives and libraries in order to produce explanations of why, or how, past events turned out the way they did. They examine the causes and consequence of human actions in times of war, revolution, civil war, or even peace. They study ideas and economies, nations and societies, cultures and mass movements. But when they do study a past crime—criminal, deception, or disaster—they enter a crime scene of the past where human agency meets modern science. They become forensic historians studying the crimes and follies of mankind.

Forensics has broadened the scope of evidence for historians, who have always been intellectual magpies, building their nests from the twigs and scraps of other disciplines—economics, anthropology, sociology, psychology, mathematics, geography, and so on. Some forensic tests seem to provide conclusive proof to validate a historical argument, whereas other tests shed little light on the problem. In some cases, forensic science provides new evidence and new experimental results. More often, science simply adds another dimension to the historical argument without end. History—like Gerasimov's facial reconstructions—remains a combination of artful *construction* of narrative, argument, and interpretation, and scientific *discovery* of new evidence, facts, and documents. Modern forensics can inform historical discussion with new evidence and tools, expanding the historian's toolbox. But historians continue to utilize forensic evidence only within the context of a larger body of interpretation and facts regarding the course of human events.

Forensics can indeed close some historical cases. Analytic chemistry decisively confirmed that van Meegeren's "Vermeers" and Kujau's "Hitler Diaries" were forgeries. Walter McCrone likewise demonstrated that the Shroud of Turin that supposedly covered the body of Christ was painted in the fourteenth century, not created in the first. Vincent Guinn's demonstration that all the bullets and bullet fragments from President Kennedy's and Governor Connally's bodies had come from Oswald's rifle helped close the Kennedy assassination case for all but the most persistent believers in a second shooter. DNA analysis and comparison with living relatives proved that Anastasia Romanov had indeed died in 1918 and that the pretender from Berlin, later living with her cats in Virginia, was no Romanov herself, but a Polish peasant. Facial reconstruction and DNA analysis also proved that the dead man in Abbottabad, Pakistan, was indeed Osama bin Laden, although, despite media excitement, the dead sister in Boston probably never existed. And cyberforensics helped convict Kevin Mitnick of being a hacker and a criminal.

More often the forensic historian gains new knowledge from new evidence without closing the case entirely. Higher than normal arsenic levels in Napoleon's hair did not necessarily mean he was murdered. Identifying the genome for the 1918 influenza virus did not entirely explain why the flu was so virulent or disappeared so suddenly. Proving that a male Jefferson fathered children by Sally Hemings did not prove that Thomas Jefferson himself was that male. But forensics does remain the enemy of conspiracy theories founded on missing or misread evidence that suits a particular belief or ideology. Forensics exposes and limits nonsense.

The media are more interested in a sensational story than a historical case, closed or open. They want a compelling story with a novel ending, and they want it now. They do not want incompleteness, indeterminacy, or ambiguity. The media cannot wait patiently until forensic historians and scientists finish their plodding work. Thus the media often rush to create a virtual reality that encourages forensic historians to publicize their findings prematurely, often without peer review. The Warren Commission rushed to judgment under political pressure about the Kennedy assassination. Publisher Rupert Murdoch compelled historian Hugh Trevor-Roper to display his ignorance in public until forensic science quickly proved that the Hitler Diaries were a forgery. The Russian and American scientists debated whether they had identified Anastasia's remains years before they actually found her body and had it exhumed. Kirsty Duncan publicized her seven Norwegian miners who died of the 1918 flu before her team's tissue culture samples had been thoroughly examined and the results published in the scientific journals. And the famous "Hitler's skull" in Moscow turned out to belong to a young woman. Osama bin Laden's dead Boston sister's brain and Kevin Mitnick went viral on the Internet long before the evidence was in.

The forensic historian is less likely to ask and answer the question "Whodunit?" than the traditional historian's question of "What happened?" The how and the why matter more than the who of agency. The evidence is more likely to consist of blood, bones, tissue, and computer hard drives than documents. Proof of identity or responsibility for a crime may be crucial to litigation in the courts, but the forensic historian above all wants to discover the truth about the past. The police want to open or close the case. The courts want justice. Forensic historians produce nonfiction, not fiction, and the tools of forensics can be a critical part of the forensic historian's toolbox. They cannot and should not rush to judgment until the bones are ready to speak, the DNA test is complete, or the computer hard drive has been thoroughly examined. Only then can the forensic historian move on to challenge and revise old explanations with new evidence about the past.

Glossary

AAFS: American Academy of Forensic Scientists

AFIP: Armed Forces Institute of Pathology, established in 1862 in Washington, DC, to analyze human remains

allele: A form of gene that may be dominant or recessive

AMS: Accelerator mass spectrometry, a technique to identify particles or carbon-date objects

anatase: A form of titanium dioxide crystal

ANL: Argonne National Laboratory, outside Chicago

antinomy: A metallic substance used in making bullets and as a traditional poison

APS: Advanced photon source, used with a nuclear reactor to determine makeup and concentration of samples

arsenic: A poison that may be fatal in acute large doses or in chronic small doses

atomic evidence: Evidence in court derived from neutron activation analysis

Bakelite: An early plastic from before World War I used to harden paint to simulate aging; used to forge allegedly old paintings

carbon-14 dating: Use of a radioactive isotope to determine the age of an object

computer hacking: Finding weaknesses in a computer system and exploiting them for profit, protest, or challenge; done by criminals (black hats) or security experts (white hats)

CT scan: Computer tomography technique used in medicine to produce images of the structure and interior of the body

CSI: Crime scene investigation, defining an off-limits area where a crime occurred and evidence may be gathered; subject of numerous television shows

cyberforensics: Since 1991 the science of computer crime, usually the presentation, identification, extraction, and documentation of computer evidence—physical, visual, and printed—to solve a crime or determine abuse of company policies

debris field: The field of remains around an object after it breaks up into pieces, as with the *Titanic*, discovered on the ocean floor in 1985

DNA fingerprinting: A process of extracting, cutting, separating, and then transferring DNA fragments to a nylon membrane between two x-ray films that will produce an autoradiograph for analysis

exhumation: Digging up a buried body for reexamination

FAA: Federal Aviation Administration, the U.S. government agency responsible for forensic investigation of aircraft accidents or incidents

facial reconstruction: A process to simulate the soft tissue around a skull with rubber pegs and a cover to re-create the face

FEA: Finite element analysis, using partial differential equations to analyze head injuries and other structural damage to a body

fluorescence: The emission of light by a substance that has absorbed radiation such as ultraviolet light

forensics: The application of science to the law in order to establish the truth about a crime

forgery: A crime, usually the creation of an object supposedly made by another person at an earlier time, as in art forgery or counterfeiting

FSS: Forensic Science Service, the British government organization for criminal investigation utilizing the tools of modern science

hacking: Using a computer to intrude upon the software and hardware of another computer without authorization. *See* computer hacking

haplotype: A combination of alleles (DNA sequences) on a chromosome that are transmitted together

hemagglutin: Chemical substance in the blood that causes red blood cells to agglutinate

HSCA: House Select Committee on Assassinations, established in 1976 to reexamine the assassination of the two Kennedy brothers and Martin Luther King

ICP-MS: Inductively coupled plasma mass spectrometer, used to identify metals and nonmetals through ion emission

long bones: Bones of the arms and legs (femur, humerus, tibia) that can help establish the age, sex, and race of a crime victim

medical examiner: A licensed physician trained in forensic pathology who performs forensic autopsies to determine the cause of death

microscopy: Study of the optical or electron magnification of tiny particles or objects

mitochondria: Small nonnuclear organelles in the cytoplasm of a cell

mitochondrial DNA (mtDNA): Nonnuclear DNA inherited from the maternal line, which is very hardy, mutates rarely, and is extremely stable over long periods of time

NAA: Neutron activation analysis, a means of determining the chemical makeup of a sample by bombarding it with neutrons from a reactor and measuring radiation emission levels

odontologist: A forensic dentist who helps identify unknown bodies by matching available x-rays, casts, or photographs of teeth with dental patterns of the victims

ORNL: Oak Ridge National Laboratory, near Knoxville, Tennessee

PCR: Polymerase chain reaction, a process that amplifies tiny bits of DNA into pieces large enough for analysis; it allows scientists to manufacture millions of samples from a single copy

ppm: Parts per million, a measure of concentration

rivet theory: The theory that inferior-quality rivets in the hull plates played a key role in the sinking of the *Titanic* in 1912

skull-face superposition: Superposing a photograph of a known person with a skull or facial reconstruction to test identity

spectroscopy: Ultraviolet spectroscopy, used to identify compounds by measuring the amount and wavelength of light emitted; can reveal the type and date of paper and ink

STRs: Short tandem repeats, base pairs of DNA chains that repeat throughout parts of the chain and are ideal for DNA fingerprinting analysis

STURP: Shroud of Turin Research Project, established to determine the date that the painting on cloth was created

tissue-thickness markers: Pegs used to mark skulls at specific points in order to reconstruct faces

trace evidence: Any hair, blood, fiber, glass, semen, or other evidence normally used to identify a victim or place a suspect at the scene of a crime

ultraviolet light: Used to compare apparently identical inks, showing which fluoresces and which fades from view

VMS: Virtual Memory System, a multitasking, multiuser Digital Equipment Company operating system developed in 1979

Wget: An online software program that enables the user to download and compress very large data files

Bibliography

Baden, Michael. *Confessions of a Medical Examiner*. New York: Ivy Books, 1989.
———. *Dead Reckoning: The New Science of Catching Killers*. New York: Simon & Schuster, 2001.
Ballard, Robert D. *The Discovery of the* Titanic. New York: Warner Books, 1987.
Bartlett, W.B. *Why the* Titanic *Sank*. Stroud, Gloucestershire, UK: Amberley, 2012.
Bass, Bill, and Jon Jefferson. *Death's Acre*. New York: Berkley Books, 2003.
Bergen, Peter. *Manhunt: The Ten-Year Search for Bin Laden from 9/11 to Abbottabad*. New York: Crown, 2012.
Cadbury, Deborah. *The Last King of France*. London: St. Martin's Press, 2002.
Chambers, G. Paul. *Head Shot: The Science behind the JFK Assassination*. New York: Prometheus Books, 2010.
Christianson, Scott. *Bodies of Evidence: Forensic Science and Crime*. Guilford, CT: Lyons Press, 2006.
Coll, Steve. *The Bin Ladens: An Arabian Family in the American Century*. New York: Penguin, 2008.
Coremans, Paul. *Van Meegeren's Faked Vermeers and de Hooghs: A Scientific Examination*. Amsterdam: J.M. Meulenhoff, 1949.
Crosby, Alfred W. *America's Forgotten Pandemic: The Influenza of 1918*. Cambridge, UK: Cambridge University Press, 2003.
Dolnick, Edward. *The Forger's Spell*. New York: HarperCollins, 2008.
Duncan, Kirsty. *Hunting the 1918 Flu*. Toronto: University of Toronto Press, 2006.
Forshufvud, Sten, and Ben Weider. *Assassination at St. Helena Revisited*. New York: John Wiley, 1995.
Garza-Valdes, Leoncio A. *The DNA of God? Newly Discovered Secrets of the Shroud of Turin*. New York: Berkley Books, 1999.
Gerasimov, M.M. *The Face Finder,* trans. A.H. Brodrick. Philadelphia: J.B. Lippincott, 1971.

Goodell, Jeff. *The Cyberthief and the Samurai. The True Story of Kevin Mitnick and the Man who Hunted Him Down.* New York: Dell Publishing, 1996.

Halpern, Samuel, et al. *Report into the Loss of the* SS Titanic*: A Centennial Reappraisal.* Stroud, Gloucestershire, UK: History Press, 2011.

Hamilton, Charles. *The Hitler Diaries: Fakes That Fooled the World.* Lexington: University Press of Kentucky, 1991.

Harris, Robert. *Selling Hitler.* New York: Pantheon, 1986.

Haugen, Peter. *Was Napoleon Poisoned? And Other Unsolved Mysteries of Royal History.* Hoboken, NJ: John Wiley, 2008.

Hawass, Zahi. *Secrets from the Sand: My Search for Egypt's Past.* New York: Harry N. Abrams, 2003.

Hawass, Zahi, et al. "Ancestry and Pathology in King Tutankhamun's Family." *Journal of the American Medical Association* 303: 7 (2010): 638–647.

Joyce, Christopher, and Eric Stover. *Witnesses from the Grave: The Stories Bones Tell.* Boston: Little, Brown, 1991.

King, Greg, and Penny Wilson. *The Fate of the Romanovs.* Hoboken, NJ: John Wiley, 2003.

King, Michael R., and Gregory M. Cooper. *Who Killed King Tut? Using Modern Forensics to Solve a 3,000-Year-Old Mystery.* Amherst, NY: Prometheus Books, 2006.

Kolata, Gina. *Flu: The Story of the Great Influenza Pandemic of 1918 and the Search for the Virus That Caused It.* New York: Simon & Schuster, 2005.

Kurland, Michael. *Irrefutable Evidence: Adventures in the History of Forensic Science.* Chicago: Ivan R. Dee, 2009.

Kurtz, Michael L. *The JFK Assassination Debates: Lone Gunman versus Conspiracy.* Lawrence: University Press of Kansas, 2006.

Lopez, Jonathan. *The Man Who Made Vermeers.* New York: Houghton Mifflin, 2009.

Manhein, Mary H. *The Bone Lady: Life as a Forensic Anthropologist.* Baton Rouge: Louisiana State University Press, 1999.

Maples, William. *Dead Men Do Tell Tales.* New York: Doubleday, 1994.

Marcella, Albert J., and Robert S. Greenfield. *Cyberforensics: A Field Manual for Collecting, Examining and Preserving Evidence of Computer Crimes.* Boca Raton, FL: CRC Press, 2002.

Martin, Russell. *Beethoven's Hair.* New York: Broadway Books, 2000.

Martin, Russell, and Linda Nibley. *The Mysteries of Beethoven's Hair.* Watertown, MA: Charlesbridge, 2009.

Massie, Robert. *The Romanovs: The Final Chapter.* New York: Random House, 1995.

McCarty, Jennifer Hooper, and Tim Foecke. *What Really Sank the* Titanic*?* New York: Kensington, 2008.

McCrone, Walter. *Judgment Day for the Shroud of Turin.* Amherst, NY: Prometheus Books, 1999.

Meadows, Anne. *Digging Up Butch and Sundance.* New York: St. Martin's Press, 1994.

Meyer, Anna. *The DNA Detectives.* New York: Thunder's Mouth Press, 2005.

Mitnick, Kevin, with William L. Simon. *Ghost in the Wires*. New York: Little, Brown, 2011.

Parenti, Michael. *History as Mystery*. San Francisco: City Lights Books, 1999.

Petrova, Ada, and Peter Watson. *The Death of Hitler: The Full Story with New Evidence from Secret Russian Archives*. New York: W.W. Norton, 1995.

Posner, Gerald. *Case Closed: Lee Harvey Oswald and the Assassination of John F. Kennedy*. New York: Random House, 1993.

Prag, John, and Richard Neave. *Making Faces: Using Forensic and Archaeological Evidence*. London: British Museum Press, 1997.

Seaver, Kirsten A. *Maps, Myths, and Men: The Story of the Vinland Map*. Stanford, CA: Stanford University Press, 2004.

Shimomura, Tsutomu, with John Markoff. *Takedown*. New York: Hyperion, 1996.

Sisman, Adam. *An Honorable Englishman: The Life of Hugh Trevor-Roper*. New York: Random House, 2010.

Skelton, R.A., Thomas E. Marston, and George D. Painter. *The Vinland Map and the Tatar Relation*. New Haven, CT: Yale University Press, 1995.

Turner, Robert F., ed. *The Jefferson-Hemings Controversy: Report of the Scholars Commission*. Durham, NC: Carolina Academic Press, 2011.

Ubelaker, Douglas, and Henry Scammel. *Bones: A Forensic Detective's Casebook*. New York: HarperCollins, 1992.

Wilcox, Robert K. *The Truth About the Shroud of Turin: Solving the Mystery*. Washington, DC: Regnery, 2010.

Williams, Robert C. *The Historian's Toolbox: A Student's Guide to the Theory and Practice of History*. 3rd edition. Armonk, NY: M.E. Sharpe, 2012.

Wrone, David R. *The Zapruder Film: Reframing JFK's Assassination*. Lawrence: University Press of Kansas, 2003.

Index

Page numbers in italics indicate photos, illustrations, and table.

A

Abbottabad, 103, 104, 105, 107, 108
Abramov, Sergei, 63
Accelerator mass spectrometry (AMS)
  defined, 123
  Joan of Arc, 30
  Shroud of Turin, 28–29
Advanced photon source (APS)
  Beethoven, Ludwig van, 48, 51
  defined, 123
  Walsh, William, 48
Afridi, Shakil, 107
Albertol, 14
Alexander the Great, 6
Allele, 123
Alvin, 93
American Academy of Forensics
    Sciences (AAFS)
  Kennedy, John, 40–41
  Last Word Society, 55–56
  members, 41, 55
American Airlines Flight 191 (1979),
    58
American Journal of Neuroradiology,
    101
America's Forgotten Pandemic
    (Crosby), 87
Analytic Chemistry, 19
Analytic chemistry
  Hitler Diaries, 24, 25–26
  Joan of Arc, 29
  Shroud of Turin, 27–29
  Vermeer forgery, 11
  Vinland Map, 18, 20

Anastasia, Grand Duchess, 62, 64, 65,
    66, 68–69, 70
Anatase
  defined, 123
  Vinland Map, 19, 20, 21
"Anderson, Anna," 62, 68–69, 70
Andropov, Yuri, 79
Antimony, 123
Antoinette, Marie, 73–74, 75, 76
Antommarchi, Francesco, 35
Argentina Forensic Anthropology
    Team (EAAF), 58
Argonne National Laboratory
    (Illinois), 48, 51–52, 123
Armed Forces Institute of Pathology
    (AFIP)
  defined, 123
  influenza epidemic (1918–1919), 87
  Kerley, Ellis, 58, 60
  Mengele, Josef, 58, 60
  Romanov family, 68
  Taubenberger, Jeffrey, 87
Arsenic
  defined, 123
  Ivan the Terrible, 7
"Arsenic Content of Napoleon I's Hair
    Probably Taken Immediately
    after His Death" (Forshufvud and
    Smith), 36
Arsenic poisoning
  Bonaparte, Napoleon, 34–38
  Taylor, Zachary, 44–48
Art of Deception, The (Mitnick), 112
Assange, Julian, 114

Assassination at St. Helena Revisited
(Weider), 37
Assassination of St. Helena
(Forshufvud and Weider), 36–37
Atomic evidence
defined, 33
discovery of, 33
See also Neutron activation analysis
(NAA)
Austen, Jane, 38
Autoradiographs, 71
Avdonin, Alexander, 63, 65
Ay, 98–99

B
Bach, Johann Sebastian, 6
Backhouse, Edmund, 25
Baden, Michael
professional experience, 41, 46,
55–56, 65
Romanov family, 64–65
Baekeland, Leo, 13
Bakelite
defined, 123
Van Meegeren, Han, 10–16
Vermeer forgery, 10–16
Bakelite Corporation, 13
Baker, James, 64
Ballistics, 39, *41t*, 42–43
Battle of Little Bighorn (Montana),
57, 58
Baumgartner, Werner, 49–50
Becke line test, 27
Beethoven, Ludwig van
advanced photon source (APS), 48,
51
cymatics, 53
DNA fingerprinting, 49
exhumation, 52
fluorescence technique, 51–52
lead poisoning, 48–53, 50
media attention, 52
mitochondrial DNA (mtDNA), 52
nascent oxygen asher, 51
neutron activation analysis (NAA),
48–53
radioimmunoassay technique, 49–50
scanning electron microscope energy
dispersion spectrometry (SEM/
EDS), 51

Beethoven, Ludwig van *(continued)*
synchrotron, 51
Walsh, William, 48–53
Beethoven's Hair (2005), 52
Beethoven's Hair (Martin), 51
Bellantoni, Nick, 78, 81–82
Bell Telephone Company, 109
Berkeley Packet Filter, 112, 113
Bezymenski, Lev, 79
Bin Laden, Abdullah, 106, 107
Bin Laden, Mohamed, 105–6, 107
Bin Laden, Osama, *106*
Abbottabad, 103, 104, 105, 107, 108
DNA fingerprinting, 103–8
facial recognition, 104–5
media attention, 103–4, 105, 107,
108
Operation Neptune Spear, 103
skull-face superposition, 104
U.S. Navy SEALS, 103–8
Birkby, Walter, 49
Bogoliubsky, Andrei, 6
Bonaparte, Napoleon, *35*
arsenic poisoning, 34–38
exhumation, 35
Forshufvud, Sten, 34–38
inductively coupled plasma-mass
spectrometry (ICP–MS), 37
neutron activation analysis (NAA),
34–38
Bone pathology
Ivan the Terrible, 7, 8–9
Louis XVII (King of France), 74–75
Mengele, Josef, 60–61
Romanov family, 63–66
Tutankhamun (King of Egypt),
99–101
See also Long-bone analysis
Borch, Gerhard ter, 12
Bormann, Martin, 25
Bossert, Liselotte, 59
Bossert, Wolfram, 59
Botkin, Evgeny S., 63–64
Braun, Eva, 78, 79
Bredius, Abraham, 12
Brennan, John, 104–5
Brier, Bob, 99–100
Brilliant, Ira, 48–49
Brinkman, Bernard, 76
British Secret Services, 24–25

Brown, Jeffrey, 52
Browning, Christopher, 82–83
Bundy, Ted, 65
Buried History, 99

C
Cahill, Thomas, 19, 20
Callender, James, 70
Carbon-14 dating
  defined, 123
  Joan of Arc, 29, 30
  Shroud of Turin, 26–29
  Vinland Map, 20
Carpathia, 92, 97
Carter, Howard, 99
Case Closed (Posner), 43
Cassidy, Butch, 57
Cassiman, Jean-Jacques
  DNA fingerprinting, 73–78
  Louis XVII (King of France),
    73–78
  media attention, 76–77
  mitochondrial DNA (mtDNA), 75,
    76, 77
  polymerase chain reaction (PCR)
    technique, 75, 76
  professional experience, 75
  publications, 75
Castro, Fidel, 44
Catholic Church
  Joan of Arc, 29–31
  Shroud of Turin, 26–29
  Vinland Map, 19–21
Center for Beethoven Studies
    (California), 49, *50*
Central Intelligence Agency (CIA),
    103, 105, 107
Chambers, G. Paul, 43
Charlier, Philippe
  accelerator mass spectrometry
    (AMS), 30
  analytic chemistry, 29
  carbon-14 dating, 29, 30
  DNA fingerprinting, 29
  Joan of Arc, 29–31
  microscopy, 29, 30
  pollen analysis, 30
Clark, Robin, 20
Coble, Michael, 69
Colbert, Stephen, 86, 97, 112

Cold Case, 56
Cold case files
  bin Laden, Osama, 103–8
  Foecke, Tim, 92–98
  Hawass, Zahi, 98–102
  influenza epidemic (1918–1919),
    86–92
  McCarty, Jennifer, 92–98
  Mitnick, Kevin, 108–15
  Shimomura, Tsutomu, 108–15
  Taubenberger, Jeffrey, 86–92
  Titanic rivet theory, 92–98
  Tutankhamun (King of Egypt),
    98–102
  U.S. Navy SEALs, 103–8
Colorimetric spectrophotometry, 47
Columbus, Christopher, 16
Comcowich, Greg, 105
Computer hacking
  defined, 124, 125
  Manning, Bradley, 114–15
  Mitnick, Kevin, 108–15
  Shimomura, Tsutomu, 108–15
  Wget software program, 114–15
  WikiLeaks, 114–15
Computer tomography (CT)
  defined, 124
  facial reconstruction, 7–8
  Tutankhamun (King of Egypt),
    98–102
Connally, John, 38, 39, 43
Cooper, Greg, 100, 101–2
Coremans, Paul
  professional experience, 11
  publications, 14
  van Meegeren, Han, 10–16
  Vermeer forgery, 10–16
Crick, Francis, 71
Crime scene investigation (CSI)
  defined, 124
  media attention, 56
Crosby, Alfred, 87
Crystallography, 18
CSI, 56
CT scan. *See* Computer tomography
    (CT)
Custer, George, 57, 58
Cyberforensics
  computer tools, 112–13,
    114–15

Cyberforensics *(continued)*
   defined, 124
   Manning, Bradley, 114–15
   Mitnick, Kevin, 108–15
   Shimomura, Tsutomu, 108–15
   Wget software program, 114–15
   WikiLeaks, 114–15
Cyberpunk (Markoff), 112
Cymatics, 53

D

Death of Adolf Hitler, The
   (Bezymenski), 79
Death of Hitler, The (Petrova and
   Watson), 80
Debris field
   defined, 124
   Titanic rivet theory, 93, 97–98
DeCarlo, Francesco, 51
De Gaulle, Charles, 30
Delorme, Philippe, 75
De Mello, José Antonio, 59
Demidova, Anna S., 63–64
Dental analysis. *See* Odontology
De Voogt, Anna, 12
DiCaprio, Leonardo, 96
Digital Equipment Corporation, 110–11
*Discoveries of the Norsemen in
   America, The* (Fischer), 20
DNA (deoxyribonucleic acid), 71
DNA fingerprinting
   allele, 123
   analysis process, 66–68, 71–72, 75,
      76, 88–89, 90
   autoradiographs, 71
   Beethoven, Ludwig van, 49
   Bin Laden, Osama, 103–8
   Cassiman, Jean–Jacques, 73–78
   defined, 124
   Foster, Eugene, 70–73
   Gill, Peter, 62–70
   haplotype, 125
   Hemings, Sally, 70–73
   Hitler's skull, 78–83
   influenza epidemic (1918–1919),
      86–92
   Ivan the Terrible, 9
   Jefferson, Thomas, 70–73
   Jeffreys, Alec, 61–62, 66, 71–72
   Joan of Arc, 29

DNA fingerprinting *(continued)*
   Louis XVII (King of France), 73–78
   Mengele, Josef, 57–62
   mitochondria, 68
   mitochondrial DNA (mtDNA), 52,
      67–68, 75, 76, 77, 81–82
   polymerase chain reaction (PCR)
      technique, 66, 75, 76, 88–89, 90
   research overview, 55–56
   Romanov family, 62–70
   Short Tandem Repeats (STR), 66
   Snow, Clyde, 57–62
   Stalin, Joseph, 9
   Strausbaugh, Linda, 78–83
   Tutankhamun (King of Egypt), 102
   variable number tandem repeats
      (VNTR), 66
Doherty, Paul, 100–1
Downs, James, 89, 90
Duncan, Kirsty, 90–91
Dyer, Frank, 47, 48

E

Eddowes, Michael, 43
Eichmann, Adolf, 59
Eisenstein, Sergei, 6
Electron micrographs
   Beethoven, Ludwig van, 51
   Shroud of Turin, 27
   Titanic rivet theory, 92, 95
Ellis, Joseph, 70, 72
Endris, Rolf, 59
Eriksson, Leif, 16
Erwin, Gerald, 99–100
European Journal of Human Genetics,
   75
Exhumation
   Beethoven, Ludwig van, 52
   Bonaparte, Napoleon, 35
   defined, 124
   Hitler's skull, 78, 79
   Ivan the Terrible, 5–6
   Mengele, Josef, 59
   Romanov family, 63–64, 69
   Taylor, Zachary, 45, 46

F

Facial recognition, 104–5
Facial reconstruction
   computer tomography (CT), 7–8

Facial reconstruction *(continued)*
  defined, 124
  by Gerasimov, Mikhail, 5–9
  of Ivan the Terrible, 5–9
  Mengele, Josef, 61
  Pizarro, 46
  Romanov family, 63, 65
  tissue-thickness markers (pegs), 6
  Tutankhamun (King of Egypt), 100
  See also Skull-face superposition
Federal Aviation Administration
    (FAA)
  American Airlines Flight 191 (1979),
    57, 58
  defined, 57
Federal Bureau of Investigation (FBI)
  Bin Laden, Osama, 103, 105, 106–8
  computer hacking, 111, 113–14
  Kennedy, John, 39–40, 42–43
Feller, Robert, 15
Ferrajoli de Ry, Enzo, 16–17
Feynman, Richard, 113
Finite element analysis (FEA)
  defined, 124
  Titanic rivet theory, 96
Fletcher, Joann, 100
Fluorescence technique
  Beethoven, Ludwig van, 51–52
  defined, 124
  Hitler Diaries, 21–26
Foecke, Tim
  electron micrographs, 92, 95
  finite element analysis (FEA), 96
  professional experience, 93–94
  publications, 96, 97
  Titanic rivet theory, 92–98
Forensics
  defined, 3, 124
  forensic historians, 3
  media attention, 56, 85–86, 121–22
  modern forensic science, 118–22
  scope of evidence, 3–5, 120–21
Forensic Science Institute, 37
Forensic Science Service (Great
    Britain), 62, 66, 124
Forgery
  Bakelite, 10–16
  Charlier, Philippe, 29–31
  Coremans, Paul, 10–16
  defined, 124

Forgery *(continued)*
  Fischer, Josef, 19–21
  fluorescence technique, 21–26
  Grant, Julius, 25–26
  Hitler Diaries, 21–26
  Joan of Arc, 29–31
  Kujau, Konrad, 23–26
  McCrone, Walter, 16–21, 26–29
  research overview, 10
  Shroud of Turin, 26–29
  van Meegeren, Han, 10–16
  Vermeer, Johannes, 10–16
  Vinland Map, 16–21
Forshufvud, Sten
  Bonaparte, Napoleon, 34–38
  hair analysis, 34–38
  neutron activation analysis (NAA),
    34–38
  odontology, 34
  professional experience, 34
  publications, 36–37
Foster, Eugene
  DNA fingerprinting, 70–73
  Hemings, Sally, 70–73
  Jefferson, Thomas, 70–73
  professional experience, 70–71
Froede, Richard, 64

G
Gacy, John Wayne, 57, 58
Gas chromatography, 15
Gatliff, Betty Pat, 46
Gear, James L., 42
Gehlen, Reinhard, 23
Gerasimov, Mikhail
  facial reconstruction
    Ivan the Terrible, 5–9
    Tamerlane, 6
  professional experience, 6
Ghost in the Wires (Mitnick), 109, 111
Gibbon, Edward, 3
Gill, Peter
  DNA fingerprinting, 62–70
  professional experience, 66
  Romanov family, 62–70
Goebbels, Joseph, 78, 79
Goebbels, Magda, 78, 79
Goebbles, Joseph, 25
Göring, Hermann, 10, 13
Greathouse, Richard, 46

Guevara, Alfredo (Che), 48–49
Guinn, Vincent
  Kennedy, John, 38–44
  neutron activation analysis (NAA),
    38–44
  professional experience, 41–42, 55–56
  radiochemistry, 41–42

H
Hackenjos, Irene, 62
Hacking. *See* Computer hacking
Hagleberg, Erika, 61–62
Hair analysis
  Bonaparte, Napoleon, 34–38
  Forshufvud, Sten, 34–38
  Louis XVII (King of France), 75, 76
  neutron activation analysis (NAA),
    34–38, 48–53
  Walsh, William, 48–53
Halliburton, Richard, 63
Hals, Franz, 12, 14
Handwriting analysis, 26
Haplotype, 125
Harland and Wolff (Ireland), 92
Harrison, R.G., 99
Hawass, Zahi, *101*
  computer tomography (CT), 98–102
  DNA fingerprinting, 102
  publications, 102
  Tutankhamun (King of Egypt), 98–102
Head Shot (Chambers), 43
Heidemann, Gerd, 23, 24, 26
Helmer, Richard, 59, 61
Hemagglutin, 125
Hemings, Eston, 72–73
Hemings, Sally, *71*
  DNA fingerprinting, 70–73
Hermit of Peking, The (Trevor-Roper),
    25
His, Wilhelm, 6
History as Mystery (Parenti), 47
Hitler, Adolf, diaries of
  analytic chemistry, 24, 25–26
  fluorescence technique, 21–26
  forgery, 21–26
  Grant, Julius, 25–26
  handwriting analysis, 26
  Kujau, Konrad, 23–26
  media attention, 21–23, 25, 26
  Trevor-Roper, Hugh, 21–26

Hitler, Adolf, skull analysis
  DNA fingerprinting, 78–83
  exhumation, 78, 79
  media attention, 78, 81
  odontology, 79, 80
  Operation Archive, 79, 80
  Operation Myth File, 80
  Strausbaugh, Linda, 78–83
Holocaust, 57–62
Hooch, Pieter de, 12
House Select Committee on
    Assassinations (HSCA)
  defined, 125
  Kennedy, John, 40–41, 42, 43,
    119–120
  Kennedy, Robert, 40–41
  King, Martin Luther, 40–41
Huckleberry Finn (Twain), 74
Hultin, Johan, 89–90, 91
Hunting the 1918 Flu (Duncan), 91

I
Inductively coupled plasma-mass
    spectrometry (ICP-MS)
  Bonaparte, Napoleon, 37
  defined, 125
Influenza epidemic (1918–1919), *88*
  DNA fingerprinting, 86–92
  H5N1 bird flu, 91
  H1N1 subtype, 88–89, 91
  media attention, 91
  Taubenberger, Jeffrey, 86–92
Iran hostage crisis (1980), 58
Ivanov, Pavel, 66–69
Ivan the Terrible, *8*
  arsenic content, 7
  bone pathology, 7, 8–9
  DNA fingerprinting, 9
  exhumation, 5–6
  facial reconstruction, 5–9
  Gerasimov, Mikhail, 5–9
  media attention, 6
  mercury content, 7

J
Jason, 93
Jefferson, Field, 72
Jefferson, Randolph, 72–73
Jefferson, Thomas
  DNA fingerprinting, 70–73

Jefferson, Thomas *(continued)*
    Foster, Eugene, 70–73
    Hemings, Sally, 70–73, 71
    media attention, 70, 72
Jeffreys, Alec, *67*
    DNA fingerprinting, 61–62, 66, 71–72
    Romanov family, 61–62, 66
Joan of Arc, *31*
    accelerator mass spectrometry
        (AMS), 30
    analytical chemistry, 29
    carbon-14 dating, 29, 30
    Charlier, Philippe, 29–31
    DNA fingerprinting, 29
    microscopy, 29, 30
    pollen analysis, 30
Johnson, Lyndon, 16, 38–39
Jones, E.H., 37
Jonestown, Guyana, 58
Jose, Maria, 17
*Journal of the American Medical
    Association*, 102

K
Kalganov, Alexander, 80
Kaplan, Lewis, 107
Kaufman, Paul, 52
Keats, John, 49–50
Keisch, Bernard, 15
Kemner, Kenneth, 51, 52
Kennedy, John
    assassination analysis, 38–44
    bullet fragments, *41*, 42–43
    conspiracy theory, 39, 43–44
    Guinn, Vincent, 38–44
    lone-gunman theory, 38–39, 43
    magic bullet, 39, 40, 43
    Mannichler-Carcano rifle, 39, 42–43
    neutron activation analysis (NAA),
        38–44
    Warren Commission, 38–39, 40
Kennedy, Robert, 40–41
Kerley, Ellis
    Iran hostage crisis (1980), 58
    Jonestown, Guyana, 58
    Mengele, Josef, 58–62
    professional experience, 41, 55–56,
        58, 60
Kharitonov, Ivan M., 63–64
Khristoforov, Vasily, 82

King, Martin Luther, 40–41
King, Mary-Claire, 68
King, Mike, 100, 101–2
Kistiakovsky, George, 41
Klein, Hans, 61–62
Klugman, Jack, 56
Knight, Alec, 69
Kodak Company, 13
Korteling, Bartus, 12
Kozlov, Vladimir, 82
Kraft, Amy, 88–89
Kujau, Konrad, *24*
    Hitler Diaries, 23–26
Kulikovsky, Tikhon, 69

L
Lachouque, Henry, 34
Lamo, Adrian, 114
Last Days of Hitler, The (Trevor–
    Roper), 25, 78–79
Last Tsar, The (Radzinsky), 65
Lead poisoning (Beethoven, Ludwig
    van), 48–53
Leiter, Michael, 104
Levine, Lowell
    Mengele, Josef, 58, 59–60, 61
    odontology, 58, 61, 65
    professional experience, 41, 46,
        55–56, 58, 65
    Romanov family, 64–65
Lincoln, Abraham, 87
London Times, 17
Long-bone analysis
    defined, 125
    Trotter, Mildred, xi–xiii, 46, 55, 58,
        61, 63
    See also Bone pathology
Los Alamos National Laboratory (New
    Mexico), 50–51, 113
Louis XVII (King of France), *77*
    bone pathology, 74–75
    Cassiman, Jean-Jacques, 73–78
    DNA fingerprinting, 73–78
    hair analysis, 75, 76
    heart preservation, 74, 75–78
    media attention, 76–77
    mitochondrial DNA (mtDNA), 75,
        76, 77
    polymerase chain reaction (PCR)
        technique, 75, 76

M

Magdeburg, Germany, 78
Mahdy, Christine El, 100–1
Manahan, Anna, 69
Manahan, Jack, 69
Mancini, Derrick, 51
Mannichler-Carcano rifle, 39, 42–43
Manning, Bradley, 114–15
Maples, William
  neutron activation analysis (NAA),
    44–48
  Pizarro, Francisco, 46, 64
  professional experience, 45–46,
    55–56, 65
  Romanov family, 46, 63, 64–65
  scope of evidence, 4
  Taylor, Zachary, 44–48, 64
Marchand, Louis, 34
Markoff, John, 111, 112
Marsh, James, 35
Martin, Russell, 51
Maser, Werner, 80
Maucher, Karl, 69
McCarty, Jennifer
  professional experience, 94
  publications, 97
  Titanic rivet theory, 92–98
McCrone, Lucy, 18
McCrone, Walter
  Becke line test, 27
  Beethoven, Ludwig van, 50
  carbon-14 dating, 27–29
  crystallography, 18
  nascent oxygen asher, 51
  polarized light microscopy, 18–19,
    20, 27
  professional experience, 18, 41
  publications, 20
  scanning electron microscope energy
    dispersion spectrometry (SEM/
    EDS), 51
  scanning electron microscope
    (SEM), 27
  Shroud of Turin, 26–29
  Vinland Map forgery, 16–21
McCrone Associates, 18
McCrone Research Institute, 51
McGreavey, Sue, 105
Media attention
  Beethoven, Ludwig van, 52

Media attention *(continued)*
  bin Laden, Osama, 103–4, 105, 107,
    108
  forensics, 56, 85–86, 121–22
  Hitler Diaries, 21–23, 25, 26
  Hitler's skull, 78, 81
  influenza epidemic (1918–1919), 91
  Ivan the Terrible, 6
  Jefferson, Thomas, 70, 72
  Louis XVII (King of France), 76–77
  Mengele, Josef, 59–60
  Mitnick, Kevin, 111–12
  Taylor, Zachary, 46
  Titanic rivet theory, 94, 97
  Vinland Map, 16–18, 19–20
Medical examiner
  defined, 125
  media attentions, 56
Mellon, Paul, 17, 20
Mengele, Josef, *60*
  bone pathology, 60–61
  DNA fingerprinting, 57–62
  exhumation, 59
  facial reconstruction, 61
  Kerley, Ellis, 58–62
  Levine, Lowell, 58, 59–60
  media attention, 59–60
  odontology, 58, 61
  skull-face superposition, 59, 61
  Snow, Clyde, 57–62
Menzies, Stewart, 25
Mercury, 7
Microscope, 20
Microscopy
  defined, 125
  Joan of Arc, 29, 30
  See also Polarized light microscopy
Miedl, Alois, 13
Mitchell, Stuart, 53
Mitnick, Kevin, *110*
  computer hacking, 108–15
  criminal background, 110–11
  cyberforensics, 108–15
  media attention, 111–12
  publications, 109, 111, 112
  Shimomura, Tsutomu, 108–15
  telephone systems, 109–11
  Virtual Memory System (VMS),
    110–11
Mitnick Security Consulting, 112

Mitochondria
defined, 125
Romanov family, 68
Mitochondrial DNA (mtDNA)
Beethoven, Ludwig van, 52
defined, 125
Hitler's skull, 81–82
Louis XVII (King of France), 75, 76, 77
Romanov family, 67–68
Moisse, Katie, 105
Mountain, Joanna, 69
Murder of Napoleon, The (Forshufvud and Weider), 36–37
Murder of Tut, The (Brier), 100
Murdoch, Rupert, 22–23, 26
Mussolini, Benito, 26

N
Nascent oxygen asher, 51
National Oceanic and Atmospheric Administration, 96
Nature, 9, 36, 37, 72, 89, 91
Naundorff, Karl Wilhelm, 74–75
Nelson, Heather, 82
Neutron activation analysis (NAA)
Beethoven, Ludwig van, 48–53
Bonaparte, Napoleon, 34–38
defined, 125
Forshufvud, Sten, 34–38
Guinn, Vincent, 38–44
hair analysis, 34–38, 48–53
Kennedy, John, 38–44
Kennedy, Robert, 40–41
King, Martin Luther, 40–41
Maples, William, 44–48
research overview, 33–34
Taylor, Zachary, 44–48
Walsh, William, 48–53
New Detectives, The, 56
New York Times, 111
Nicholas II, Tsar, 62–64, 68
Nichols, George, II, 46, 47, 48
Nichols, John, 42

O
Oakes, Catherine, 64–65
Oak Ridge National Laboratory (ORNL)
Kennedy, John, 40
Taylor, Zachary, 44, 47–48

Obama, Barack, 103, 104
O'Connor, Craig, 82
Odontology
American Airlines Flight 191 (1979), 58
defined, 125
Forshufvud, Sten, 34
Hitler's skull, 79, 80
human rights abuses, 58
Levine, Lowell, 58, 61, 65
Mengele, Josef, 58, 61
Romanov family, 65
Taylor, Zachary, 47
Oetzi the Iceman, 118, *119*
On Trial, Lee Harvey Oswald, 42
Operation Archive, 79, 80
Operation Myth File, 80
Operation Neptune Spear, 103
Ortner, Donald, 61
Oswald, Lee Harvey, 38–39, 42, 43–44

P
Pacific Bell Company, 110
Panetta, Leon, 104
Parenti, Michael, 47–48
Particle-Induced X-Ray Emission (PIXE), 19
Pellatan, Philippe-Jean, 74
Petri, Hans, 75
Petrova, Ada, 80
Philip, Prince (Duke of Edinburgh), 62, 67
Pizarro, Francisco, 46, 64
Pogony, Yakov, 80
Polarized light microscopy
Shroud of Turin, 27
Vinland Map, 18–19, 20
Pollen analysis, 30
Polymerase chain reaction (PCR) technique
defined, 125
influenza epidemic (1918–1919), 88–89, 90
Louis XVII (King of France), 75, 76
Romanov family, 66
Posner, Gerald, 43
PPM (parts per million), 126
Prokapenko, Anatolii, 80

Q

Quincy, M.E., 56

R

Radiochemistry, 41–42
Radioimmunoassay technique, 49–50
Radzinsky, Eduard, 65
Raman microscopy, 20
Reid, Ann, 90–91
Rembrandt Society, 12
Richards, Robin, 100
Rinaldi, Peter, 27
Rising, Clara, 44–45, 48
Rivet theory. *See Titanic* rivet theory
Robinson, Larry, 47
Romanov family, *64*
  Aleksei, 62, 64, 65, 66, 69
  Alexandra, 62, 63–64
  Anastasia, 62, 64, 65, 66, 68–69, 70
  bone pathology, 63–66
  DNA fingerprinting, 62–70
  Elizabeth, 69
  exhumation, 63–64, 69
  facial reconstruction, 63, 65
  George, 68
  Gill, Peter, 62–70
  Kulikovsky, Tikhon, 69
  Maples, William, 46, 63, 64–65
  Marie, 63–64
  Nicholas II, 62–64, 68
  odontology, 65
  Olga, 63–64
  Philip (Duke of Edinburgh), 62, 67
  Tatiana, 63–64
Roosevelt, Franklin D., 30
Roosevelt, Theodore, 20
Ryabov, Geli, 63, 65

S

Scanning electron microscope energy
    dispersion spectrometry (SEM/
    EDS), 51
Scanning electron microscope (SEM), 27
Schanzkowska, Francisca, 68–69
Schofield, Bertram, 17
Science, 89, 91
Scope of evidence
  case elements, 3–4
  forensic historians, 3
  forensics, 3–5, 120–21

Season of the Wild Rose (Rising),
    44–45
Seaver, Kirsten, 19–20
Semenovsky, Pyotr, 79
Shaver, David, 114
Shimomura, Tsutomu
  computer hacking, 108–15
  Mitnick, Kevin, 108–15, 112
  professional experience, 113
Short Tandem Repeats (STR)
  defined, 126
  Romanov family, 66
Shroud of Turin, *28*
  accelerator mass spectrometry
    (AMS), 28–29
  analytic chemistry, 27–29
  Becke line test, 27
  carbon-14 dating, 26–29
  McCrone, Walter, 26–29
  polarized light microscopy, 27
  scanning electron microscope
    (SEM), 27
Shroud of Turin Research Project
    (STURP), 27, 126
Skull-face superposition
  bin Laden, Osama, 104
  defined, 126
  Mengele, Josef, 59, 61
  See also Facial reconstruction
SKULLpture Inc., 46
Smith, Hamilton, 34, 36
Snow, Clyde
  American Airlines Flight 191 (1979),
    57, 58
  Battle of Little Bighorn (Montana),
    57, 58
  Cassidy, Butch, 57
  DNA fingerprinting, 57–62
  Gacy, John Wayne, 57, 58
  human rights abuses, 57, 58
  media attention, 59–60
  Mengele, Josef, 57–62
  professional experience, 41, 55–56,
    57–58
  Sundance Kid, 57
Sognanaes, Reidar, 80
Sonar imaging, 96, 97–98
Spectroscopy, 126
Spillsbury, Bernard, 65
Stalin, Joseph, 5–6, 9

Stella Matutina (Austria), 20–21
Stern, 21–22, 23, 25
Strausbaugh, Linda
    DNA fingerprinting, 78–83
    Hitler's skull, 78–83
    professional experience, 82
STURP (Shroud of Turin Research
    Project), 27, 126
Subbottom profiling, 96
Sundance Kid, 57
Sunday Times, 22–23
Syes, Mark, 91
Synchrotron, 51

T
Takedown (Shimomura and Markoff),
    112
Tamerlane, 6
Tatar Relation, The, 16, 17, 19–20
Taubenberger, Jeffrey
    influenza epidemic (1918–1919),
      86–92
    polymerase chain reaction (PCR)
      technique, 88–89, 90
    professional experience, 87
    publications, 91
Taylor, Eva, 17
Taylor, Zachary, *45*
    arsenic poisoning, 44–48
    colorimetric spectrophotometry, 47
    exhumation, 45, 46
    Maples, William, 44–48, 64
    media attention, 46
    neutron activation analysis (NAA),
      44–48
    odontology, 47
Taylor File, The (Rising), 48
Teestov, Anna, 18
Thatcher, Margaret, 25
Tillos, Jean-Henri, 74
Time, 13
Tissue-thickness markers (pegs)
    defined, 126
    facial reconstruction, 6
Titanic (1997), 96
Titanic rivet theory
    debris field, 93, 97–98
    defined, 126
    electron micrographs, 92, 95
    finite element analysis (FEA), 96

Titanic rivet theory *(continued)*
    Foecke, Tim, 92–98
    McCarty, Jennifer, 92–98
    media attention, 94, 97
    sonar imaging, 96, 97–98
    subbottom profiling, 96
Todd, Albert C., 52
Toma, Romeu, 59
Tooth analysis. *See* Odontology
Toscas, George, 107
Trace evidence, 126
Trevor-Roper, Hugh
    Hitler Diaries, 21–26
    Kennedy, John, 39
    publications, 25, 78–79
Tristan, Charles, 37
Trotter, Mildred, *xii*
    long-bone analysis, xi–xiii, 46, 55,
      58, 61, 63
Trupp, Aleksei I., 63–64
Turner, Robert F., 72
Tutankhamun (King of Egypt)
    bone pathology, 99–101
    computer tomography (CT), 98–102
    DNA fingerprinting, 102
    facial reconstruction, 100
    Hawass, Zahi, 98–102
Twain, Mark, 74

U
Ultraviolet light
    defined, 126
    Hitler Diaries, 26
    See also Fluorescence technique
Umberto II (King of Italy), 10, 27
U.S. Army Central Identification
    Laboratory (Hawaii), xi–xii, 46,
      65, 69
U.S. Department of Justice, 59
U.S. Marshals Service, 58, 59
U.S. Navy SEALs, 103–8

V
Van Meegeren, Han
    Bakelite, 10–16
    Christ with the Adultress, 13
    Coremans, Paul, 10–16
    forgery techniques, 12–16
    Gentleman and the Lady at the
      Spinet, The, 12–13

Van Meegeren, Han *(continued)*
  Hals forgery, 12, 13–14
  paint pigments, 12, 13, 14, 15, 15–16
  personal background, 11–12
  Supper at Emmaus, The, 12
  Vermeer forgery, 10–16
*Van Meegeren's Faked Vermeers and
  de Hooghs* (Coreman), 14
Variable number tandem repeats
  (VNTR), 66
Vaughn, Roscoe, 89, 90
Vermeer, Johanness, 10–16
Vinland Map, *18*
  analytic chemistry, 18, 20
  anatase, 19, 20, 21
  carbon-14 dating, 20
  Fischer, Josef, 19–21
  forgery, 16–21
  ink pigments, 19, 20, 21
  McCrone, Walter, 16–21
  media attention, 16–18, 19–20
  Particle-Induced X-Ray Emission
    (PIXE), 19
  polarized light microscopy, 18–19, 20
  Raman microscopy, 20
  Tatar Relation, The, 16, 17, 19–20
  "Vinland Map, The" (McCrone), 20

W
Wallis, Helen, 17, 19, 29
Walsh, William
  advanced photon source (APS), 48
  Beethoven, Ludwig van, 48–53
  hair analysis, 48–53
  neutron activation analysis (NAA),
    48–53
  professional experience, 50–51

Ward, Michael, 47
Warren, Earl, 38–39
Warren Commission, 38–39, 40
Washington University Medical
  School, xi
Wassenbergh, H.A., 14
Watson, James, 71
Watson, Peter, 80
Weider, Ben, 36–37
Werner, Louis Ferdinand, 25
Wget software program
  computer hacking, 114–15
  defined, 126
What Really Sank the Titanic (Foecke
  and McCarty), 97
White, Dick, 25
White Star Line, 92
Who Killed Napoleon? (Forshufvud),
  36
WikiLeaks, 114–15
Williams, Eleazar, 74
Winslet, Kate, 96
Winsor and Newton, 15–16
Witten, Laurence C., 16–17
Woods Hole Oceanographic Institute
  (Massachusetts), 93, 113
Woodson, Thomas, 72, 73

Y
Yale University Press, 16–18, 19–20
Yurovsky, Yakov, 63, 65

Z
Ziagin, Victor, 80

About the Author

Robert C. Williams is Vail Professor of History and Dean of Faculty Emeritus at Davidson College in Davidson, North Carolina. He is the author of numerous books and articles in modern Russian, European, and American history, and a founding member of History Associates Incorporated. He has also taught history at Williams College, Washington University in St. Louis, and Bates College. He and his wife Ann live in Center Lovell, Maine, where he persists in doing history.